1971

Hawthorne, the Artist

Hawthorne, the Artist
FINE-ART DEVICES IN FICTION

———◆◆———

Leland Schubert

NEW YORK
RUSSELL & RUSSELL · INC

TO

Helen Stockdale Dwan

Preface

————•••————

THE following study of Hawthorne deals only with form.
I have not considered content. In "The Wayside," the introduction to *The Tanglewood Tales,* Hawthorne speaks of
certain stories as being "better chosen and better handled"
than others, and here, I think, he is talking about form, as
opposed to content. While these two elements of a work of
art are rarely separated—and usually should not be separated
—they are nevertheless separable. For the sake of analysis,
and consequently better understanding, the separation is
desirable.

Most critics and aestheticians, perhaps all of them, will
agree that to be good a work of art must be harmonious,
rhythmical, and balanced. It must have pattern and design.
Although criticism in the fields of graphic and plastic art
and music has much to say about form, literary criticism
(particularly of prose) often gives very little stress to it. This
is notably true, I think, in Hawthorne criticism. It is with
this element in the art of Hawthorne, *form,* that the present
study is concerned.

Not in what Hawthorne says in his stories and novels—
not necessarily, even, in the way he says it are we interested
here. Our interest is in his medium and his use of that medium, in his *means of achieving results.* We shall look at his
words, his groups of words (phrases, sentences, paragraphs,
and chapters), and his over-all massing of words (the stories
and novels) to see how he employs them as artistic devices,
not as rhetorical devices. We shall analyze Hawthorne's writing and criticize it as we would the work of any other artist,
whether a painter, a sculptor, or even a musician. (But we

shall not be concerned with the meaning of the devices. That is a matter of symbolism, and consequently of content.) Hawthorne's purpose, his method, and, as we shall see later, his means are similar to those of non-literary artists. We shall devote ourselves in this study to discovering those means by which Hawthorne, the artist, transfers his material from nature to art. In short, this study is *art* criticism, perhaps, rather than literary criticism.

One cannot read Hawthorne without being conscious of a tremendous emotional effect. An analysis of this almost always reveals the author's use of artistic devices usually restricted to the other arts, the non-literary arts. There is no really good reason why writers should not use such devices; in fact, most of the good ones do. Neither is there any reason why the literary analyst or critic should not fall back on the analytical method and the critical vocabulary of the so-called art critic—a term which has come to refer only to the critic of graphic and plastic art—or the music critic.

Many things which I should like to say about different aspects of Hawthorne's writing—plot, characters, morals, meanings—do not belong in this study. I have tried to stay close to form. I have taken my examples from less than half of Hawthorne's published works: *Twice Told Tales, Mosses from an Old Manse, The Scarlet Letter, The House of the Seven Gables, The Snow Image, The Blithedale Romance,* and *The Marble Faun,* with the note-books thrown in for reference and corroboration. Within these volumes, for the most part, I have considered only stories which are definitely narrative, stories which show individual characters moving through progressive plots. Consequently, I have omitted the essays, sketches, and those panoramas which I call frieze-stories. Perhaps I should apologize for the number and length of direct quotations from Hawthorne. They can be justified, I think, on the ground that discussions of art, to be most accurate and useful, should be copiously illustrated. It has not been my intention to repeat the plots of Hawthorne's stories

further than is necessary to bring out the artistic devices
under consideration. Sometimes this has demanded quite a
bit of narration, and sometimes very little. I have assumed
that the reader is acquainted with the stories.

There have appeared many lives of Hawthorne, and many
critical accounts which treat him as a writer, a thinker, a
moralist, a Puritan, a New Englander, a lonely man, or an
associate of Emerson, Thoreau, or Melville; but none that
I know of treats him exclusively as an artist. A few critics
and historians suggest the things I have tried to develop.
Henry James, in *Hawthorne* (1879), points out several of his
artistic devices; Lewis E. Gates, in a short chapter in *Studies
and Appreciations* (1900), has perhaps the most appreciative
attitude toward Hawthorne's artistry; F. O. Matthiessen, in
his *American Renaissance* (1941), touches on the subject but
does not expand it as fully as his insight and reading lead me
to believe he could. A master's thesis, "Hawthorne, a Puritan
Artist" (Cornell University, 1939), written by my wife, Helen
Dwan Schubert, is a very full account of Hawthorne's background as an artist in New England. It was this paper which
first aroused my interest in the present subject. To Mrs.
Schubert and her thesis I owe more than I can ever express.
I have tried, in the study which follows, to go on from where
these writers left off. I have tried not only to *say* that Hawthorne is an artist—in his use of structure, of line, mass,
movement, contrast, variety, rhythm, color, sound, and so on
—but also, by many illustrative examples, to *show* that he is
an artist.

I should like to thank several men who, in one way or
another, have helped produce this book. Mr. Frederick B.
Prescott and Mr. Henry A. Myers (both of Cornell Univer-
sity) and Mr. Tremaine MacDowall (University of Minne-
sota) read the manuscript in its early stages. Mr. Raymond
Adams (University of North Carolina) and Mr. J. B. Hubbell
(Duke University) read a later version. Mr. Conrad T. Logan
(Madison College) gave assistance and encouragement from

beginning to end, particularly at the time of proof-reading. Mr. David Jaffe of the University of North Carolina Press aided in carrying the project from manuscript to book. For the good suggestions and helpful criticism of each of these men I am sincerely grateful. And finally, I thank the Houghton Mifflin Company for permission to use numerous passages from the authorized edition of Hawthorne's writings.   L. S.

Contents

---

1. Introduction

"It is always difficult, and in a certain sense unnatural, to make a sharp separation between the elements of content and form. The artist himself rarely attempts it. He 'thinks in color' or feels in terms of musical sound. The finer the work of art, the more indissolubly are the elements fused through the personality of the artist. And yet it is often of the greatest value to the student to attempt this separate analysis,—to distinguish what has gone into the work of art from the external form in which it was clothed,— and in prose fiction form and content are more easily separable than in poetry or music or even painting."—BLISS PERRY, *A Study of Prose Fiction.*

NATHANIEL HAWTHORNE has often been called an artist. F. O. Matthiessen says that he is "our one major artist in fiction yet to have come out of new England"; Brander Matthews calls him "the most accomplished artist in fiction America has yet produced"; Ludwig Lewisohn classes him with Poe as an acutely conscious literary artist.[1] If Hawthorne is an artist, his products are works of art and can be looked at, analyzed, and discussed as any other works of art. In the pages that follow, some of the principles of painting, sculpture, architecture, and music will be applied to Hawthorne's writing.

It must be remembered at the outset that art is not nature,

---

[1] F. O. Matthiessen, *American Renaissance* (New York, Oxford University Press, 1941), p. 229; Brander Matthews, *An Introduction to the Study of American Literature* (New York, American Book Co., 1896), p. 123; Ludwig Lewisohn, *Expression in America* (New York, Harper and Brothers, 1932), p. 236.

Also, see John Macy, *The Spirit of American Literature* (Garden City, Doubleday, Page and Co., 1913), pp. 83, 94; Bliss Perry, *The Amateur Spirit* (Boston, Houghton Mifflin Co., 1904), pp. 123, 127; D. H. Lawrence, *Studies in Classic American Literature* (New York, Albert and Charles Boni, 1930), p. 254; George E. Woodberry, *Nathaniel Hawthorne, How to Know Him* (Indianapolis, Bobbs-Merrill Co., 1918), p. 90.

an obvious fact that is often overlooked. The true artist does not attempt to make something which is natural but, in one sense, something which is unnatural or, as we often term it, artificial. Hawthorne's stories are frequently prefaced or put in frames, and the prefaces and frames are admissions that what follows or what is included is not real but artificial, not fact but fiction. "Wakefield," for example, begins with a reference to a newspaper article. The author does not recall the story accurately, but remembers merely an outline of it. He tells us that the incident about which he once read made a sharp impression on his mind. He then goes on to say:

> Whenever any subject so forcibly affects the mind, time is well spent in thinking of it. If the reader choose, let him do his own meditation; or if he prefer to ramble with me through the twenty years of Wakefield's vagary, I bid him welcome...[1, 173][2]

Hawthorne then asks, "What sort of man was Wakefield?" He answers his own question and begins the actual story by saying: "We are free to shape our own idea and call it by his name." The shaping of Hawthorne's idea makes up the tale. It is a story, a fiction, and hence, at least to that extent, it is a work of art. In "Dr. Heidegger's Experiment" the author frankly confesses that he is responsible for some of the "fantastic stories" told about Dr. Heidegger and he admits that he "must be content to bear the stigma of fiction-monger." When he labels his stories "parable," "fantasy," "morality," "apologue," or "legend," as he so often does, he is admitting that the tales are not representations of life. At most they are presentations of what might be life-like. The stories of Hester Prynne, the ambitious guest, or Mr. Higginbotham, no less than those of Beatrice Rappaccini, Goodman Brown, or Owen Warland, are, because they are not real but artificial,

---

[2] *The Complete Writings of Nathaniel Hawthorne*, 22 vols. (Old Manse Edition; Boston, Houghton Mifflin Co., 1900). This and all following excerpts from Hawthorne are from the above edition. Specific sources will be indicated only for relatively long or important passages, and will be noted only by reference to volume and page.

within the realm of art and are therefore potential works of art. As works of art—rather than works of nature—they have selected content and arranged form. They are composed with a particular order of events and a particular arrangement of words.

Hawthorne was not a realist, although he might have been if he had known how or if he had lived at a different period in literary history.[3] There is no doubt that he admired realism in art. He liked the Dutch masters for their realistic detail and says in the note-books (1857), "Even the photograph cannot equal their miracles." [xxi, 38-39] But he knew, or at least suspected, that this was a weakness in his judgment; a year later he wrote: "It is a sign, I presume, of a taste still very defective, that I take singular pleasure in the elaborate imitations of Van Mieris, Gerard Dow, and the other old Dutch wizards . . ." Then he goes on to describe brass pots so painted "that you could see your face in them" and crockery pots "that will surely hold water." [xxii, 93] He was convinced that "a picture ought to have something in common with what the spectator sees in nature." [xxi, 114] All through *The Marble Faun* it is apparent that, in the eyes of his characters, realistic likeness is the goal of art. There is not, to my way of thinking, a truly sound bit of art criticism in the entire novel. If a thing is pretty and if it looks natural, Miriam, Hilda, and Kenyon ask no more of it. And this, I think we may believe, was essentially Hawthorne's opinion, too. In practice, he is keenly aware of form in art; in looking at other artists' work, he apparently saw only content.

In spite of a limited knowledge of the other arts and a poorly developed taste, Hawthorne shows considerable interest in art. He was well aware of the relationships between the various arts and often thought of his own in terms of others. In his note-books, for example, he asks: "Can the

---

[3] Henry James says that Hawthorne "was not in the least a realist—he was not to my mind enough of one."—*Hawthorne* (New York, Harper and Brothers, 1879), p. 65.

tolling of the Old South bell be painted?" [xvii, 301] (This
as early as 1841 when his ideas on art were in a very nebulous
stage!) Some years later he states: "The gate of a city might
be a good locality for a chapter in a novel, or for a little
sketch by itself, whether by painter or writer."[4] [xxii, 209]

Art is art, regardless of the medium. We have too long in-
sisted on separating the various forms of art; we have overlooked their obvious kinship. Hawthorne recognizes this
when he points out, in *The Marble Faun,* that the criticism
of artists who use other media is worth a great deal. One art
throws light on another. John Dewey conveys this idea when
he says "If art is an intrinsic quality of activity, we cannot
divide and subdivide it."[5] We have tended to do just this. We
have tended to say that El Greco has no business with melody
because melody is music and El Greco is painting; that
Chopin has no business with color because color is painting
and Chopin is music; or that Hawthorne has no business
with plasticity because plasticity is sculpture and Hawthorne
is prose. Even more damaging than such statements are those
that forbid the analysis of Hawthorne in terms of plasticity,
or Chopin in terms of color, or El Greco in terms of melody.
If such an analysis will increase our understanding of these
artists, will increase our appreciation for them, it should
certainly be made. The arts are not far apart. In fact, they
are amazingly close together. They are very similar, not in
their contents or their methods or their media, but in the
means by which they achieve emotional impact on their
respective observers. Schiller saw this more than a hundred
years ago:

> . . . it is a natural and necessary consequence of their per-
> fection, that, without confounding their objective limits, the
> different arts come to resemble each other more and more, in
> the action *which they exercise on the mind*. At its highest
> degree of ennobling, music ought to become a form, and act

---

[4] Other comments on the relationship between the various arts are found in
III, 246; VII, xxi, 193-4; VIII, 2; XVIII, 249; XXI, 285; and XXII, 77.
[5] *Art as Experience* (New York, Minton, Balch and Co., 1934), p. 214.

upon us with the calm power of an antique statue; in its most elevated perfection, the plastic art ought to become music and move us by the immediate action exercised on the mind by the senses; in its most complete development, poetry ought both to stir us powerfully like music and like plastic art to surround us with a peaceful light.[6]

It is in *"the action which they exercise on the mind"* that the different arts have so much in common. They all use the same means of doing this, images. The words on a page no less than the colors of a painting or the sounds of a musical composition stimulate the mind of the observer and produce various images, in terms of the observer's knowledge and experience. The emotional reaction, if any, then arises. It is the direct result of the stimulus which is composed of words or lines or colors or sounds or whatever the medium happens to be.

Let us look for a moment at a passage from Hawthorne, the opening paragraph of "The Minister's Black Veil." We shall see that the words on the page, which are static, colorless, and lifeless, will produce in our minds images which have movement, color, and life.

> The sexton stood in the porch of the Milford meeting-house, pulling busily at the bell-rope. The old people of the village came stooping along the street. Children, with bright faces, tripped merrily beside their parents, or mimicked a graver gait, in the conscious dignity of their Sunday clothes. Spruce bachelors looked sidelong at the pretty maidens, and fancied that the Sabbath sunshine made them prettier than on weekdays. When the throng had mostly streamed into the porch, the sexton began to toll the bell, keeping his eye on the Reverend Mr. Hooper's door. The first glance of the clergyman's figure was the signal for the bell to cease its summons. [1, 40]

We are not interested in this account simply as an example of action in narrative writing, though an analysis of it reveals more action than is customary in an opening paragraph.

---

[6] "Letters upon Aesthetic Education of Man," letter XXII, *Harvard Classics*, Vol. XXXII (New York, P. F. Collier and Sons, 1910), p. 285.

These lines are graphic; they paint pictures, and moving-pictures at that. We see the sexton; we locate him on the porch; then we see him busily pulling the bell-rope. In another part of the picture people are coming to church. First there are old people. Hawthorne tells us that they are old and then he shows us that they are old: they "came stooping along the street." Children occupy another part of the scene. They "tripped merrily beside their parents," or imitated their more serious manner. We can see the bachelors looking "side-long at the pretty maidens." Our eyes are carried back then to the sexton. When most of the parishioners have arrived, he begins to pull the bell-rope more slowly and he turns his head to the door of the minister's house. The busy pulling of the rope shifts to a tolling, and the sexton will stop entirely as soon as he glimpses the minister. The whole paragraph, well-rounded and complete, is a picture. It is quiet, but it is alive. It is visible, a good example of Hawthorne's graphic writing.

It is more than graphic; it is plastic. It has three dimensions. We see not just a series of figures moving across a flat canvas, but figures moving in space. Hawthorne does this in a rather obvious but none the less effective manner. He shows us the porch and the sexton. He leads our glance to the old people in the street. Here is another setting. The street with the people on it is a spatial entity, three-dimensional. The people are not just standing there; they are moving. The street is probably in front of the church-porch, and thus the picture acquires depth. When the church-goers move onto the porch, they move not horizontally across the picture, nor vertically up and down the picture, but *into* it. In this paragraph Hawthorne has given us not merely some words on a page; he has given us a picture.

Without going into an involved psychological discussion, we can safely say that the picture which we see is not on the page but in our minds. It has, however, been brought into being, or as we say, stimulated, by what is on the page. The same sort of thing happens when we look at a painting. The picture exists for us not on the wall but in our minds. On the wall are some pigments which have been carefully spread on a piece of canvas. If they have been arranged with sufficient care and with a sound idea behind their arrangement, they will stimulate our minds to produce an image. That image is in our minds, not on the canvas. The truth of this theory could be proven, perhaps, by reference to individual differences between observers: optical differences; differences in experience, background, intelligence; and other psychological elements. But to take the time and space for such proof, here, would be beside the point.

When Hawthorne or any other imaginative writer presents a series of descriptive details, he seems to proceed from a picture in his own mind (or an interpretation of life or nature, if that is a better way of saying it). He works out a group of language symbols which will evoke in the reader's mind ideas or feelings equivalent to those in his own mind. He arranges these symbols, or stimuli, according to some plan which will assure the most accurate results as well as the greatest artistic effectiveness. Words, black marks on paper (the tools of the writer), suggest to the observer, the reader, images with life, color, shape, and movement. Suggestiveness, as Hawthorne notes in *The Marble Faun,* is the highest merit of art. [x, 237] Words, in prose, constitute the suggestions. The writer, the painter, the sculptor, and the musician work in essentially the same way except that their media are different.

A musician, working out the pattern of a symphonic movement, for example, strives to get unity of impression, a single emotional impact. His artistry leads him to repeat themes which carry the feeling he is trying to convey. He often achieves an emotional surge by shifting the key or varying the tempo. He brings his major mood into sharper focus by a contrast in which he departs from his theme. He subtly blends from one melody to another or from one key to another. The musical composer sometimes divides his movement into three parts, using the middle part for contrast. He builds the whole according to a pattern which may be almost architectural, just as a dramatist builds a play, or a painter a picture, or a sculptor a statue. The playwright uses foreshadowing, sometimes called "signposts," to strengthen the force of subsequent detail. The painter repeats colors and the musician repeats motifs for the same purpose. The pattern which these various artists use is designed to support an emotion or a series of related emotions. The plan which the architect designs for the construction of a building is intended (it sometimes fails) to hold the building together, to declare its purpose and to serve that purpose, and to unify the parts in an artistic whole. This, really, is the object of any pattern in art, whether it be architecture, music, painting, sculpture—or the short-story or novel.

In the next chapter we shall look carefully at the structure of some of Hawthorne's stories, but a brief glance at the pattern of "The Maypole of Merry Mount" will be useful now. The story falls into three parts. The first and third parts, which carry the incident itself, are approximately equal in length. The middle part, which gives the historical background, is a little shorter.[7] In part one the author presents a fairly gay and colorful picture. He describes the setting and characters and states the situation. There is music and dancing and general gayety. The conversation between Edgar and Edith reveals the mystery, the foreboding in the girl's heart; and we learn that they are both "sensible of something vague and unsubstantial in their former pleasures." [1, 70] The second part of the story is a kind of interlude. We are told of the founding of Merry Mount and of its organization and purpose. It is here that Hawthorne discourses on the opposition between the "men of Iron," as he calls the Puritans,

---

[7] The number of lines: part one, 153 lines; part two, 126 lines; part three, 161 lines. The fact that the number of lines varies in different editions does not, of course, alter the proportions.

and the revelers. "After these authentic passages from history, we return to the nuptials of the Lord and Lady of the May," Hawthorne writes. [1, 75] This statement brings us back to the story again, the third part. The Puritans who dominated the historical survey of part two literally enter the picture at this point. About half the lines in part three consist of dialogue between Endicott, his henchmen, and the principals at the wedding. The Maypole is cut down, the revelers are captured, and presumably the spirit of mirth is driven out of New England.

Part two I have called an interlude. Hawthorne the historian interrupts Hawthorne the story-teller for a two-fold purpose: to give the background and to create suspense. The first part concludes with the note of "dreary presentiment." After the interlude comes the denouement. The mood of the entire story is consistent, but there is a different spirit in each of the two main parts. Whereas the first part is colorful, light, and gay, the third part is colorless, dark, and sad. Approximately eighty-five percent of the imagery in the first part consists of figures which suggest color and gayety, while in the last part only about thirty percent are of this type. Furthermore, about seventy percent of all the color and light-and-shade imagery in the story is in the first part. Percentages prove very little in literary analysis; it is the total *effect* that counts. But percentages do suggest the way in which the author's effect is achieved. By avoiding lively and colorful images, Hawthorne makes the last part of the story dark and sad. He substitutes, in part three, direct conversation which is emotional, but in an argumentative rather than a poetic way.

The pattern of "The Maypole of Merry Mount," then, is seen to be an arrangement based in part on the arrangement of images. Ultimately the pattern is an arrangement of words, but the words are chosen for their emotional value, and grouped for their emotional value, and built into a whole for their emotional value. As was stated before, the pattern is designed to support an emotion or a series of related emotions. Within the pattern, as we have seen, are a number of suggestive details. In this story the details are composed of images which seem to be the result of carefully chosen and arranged words. In a painting, the images are the result of carefully chosen and arranged colors. In music, of sounds.

Thus, in one sense, we are talking about rhetoric. But in so far as rhetoric is largely a matter of logic rather than feeling, we are, in this study, considering Hawthorne's art rather than his rhetoric. We are trying to analyze the author's means of achieving emotional effects. To us, at present, Hawthorne's words (tools of rhetoric, it is true) are vehicles of feeling rather than meaning. They are his means of arousing emotional impressions.

Sometimes, in the fiction of Hawthorne, the devices used to build up the total impression are small: suggestions repeated throughout a story; brief descriptions of sound or color or movement; rhythmically repeated notes of color, or personality traits, or ideas. Sometimes the devices are large: contrasting settings; large architectural elements; whole situations repeated or contrasted. But always two things dominate the art of Hawthorne as they dominate all art: rhythm and contrast.[8] And in his best work, structure, or pattern, is clearly seen when it is looked for. In most of his works, Hawthorne used all the tricks, all the devices, all the *means* used in the best work of all artists.

Pattern in poetry is obvious; so are rhythm, color-imagery, sound-imagery, and the repetition of figures. In some prose these devices are obvious, too. They can be found in Fielding, Irving, Scott—from whom Hawthorne doubtless learned much—as well as in Poe, Galsworthy, or Marquand. Hawthorne had access to the fine writers who wrote before him. His success in story-telling is unquestionably as much the result of literary skill as of artistic skill. It would be absurd (and

---

[8] Woodberry calls "The Christmas Banquet" one of Hawthorne's "most artistically conceived" stories: "The tale is carefully composed, especially in those points of keeping [harmony], balance, and contrast in which Hawthorne was expert . . ."
—George E. Woodberry, *Nathaniel Hawthorne* (Boston, Houghton Mifflin Co., 1902), p. 143.

quite apart from the purpose of this study) to isolate Hawthorne from his fellow-writers. If he, more than most prose writers, used some of the means used by painters, sculptors, and musicians (as I believe he did), it does not mean that he was less of a writer than some, but only more of an artist.

It is frankly and frequently admitted throughout this book that Hawthorne knew comparatively little about the other arts. His taste was often feeble and his judgment not always sound. His knowledge was not equal to his interest. In spite of this, he used numerous artistic devices. There is no dilemma here, however. He was interested in art and, what is more important, he had the sensitivity, the awareness, the mind and emotions of an artist. I do not think he copied his methods from other artists. They sprang naturally from his artistic personality. If this study seems to ignore Hawthorne the writer in its emphasis on Hawthorne the artist it is because I believe the writer has been often considered while the artist has been neglected. Although he was well versed in the use of words for their rhetorical value, he also knew how to use words for their artistic value. There is no need to defend or explain Hawthorne's rhetorical or literary skill; but there does appear to be some sense in explaining his *artistic* skill, in showing how he achieved his effects by the use of artistic devices not usually regarded as tools of the writer.

There is, of course, much more to art and to Hawthorne than structure, design, rhythm, color, light-and-shade, sound, and the other devices discussed here. There are truth and significance and humanity, which we like to call universality. It is neither desirable nor accurate to deny the presence—the very important presence—of these qualities in any work of art. They are present in Hawthorne's writings and they contribute much to the greatness of *The Scarlet Letter, The House of the Seven Gables,* "Rappaccini's Daughter," and "Ethan Brand." But these qualities have often been discussed before and they are not the whole of Hawthorne's art. Form is as much a component of art as content is. No more, perhaps, but as much.

2. *Structure*

"But form, to express itself aesthetically, must be composed; and here we touch the controlling basis of all art:—organization. Organization is the use put to form for the production of rhythm."—WILLARD HUNTINGTON WRIGHT, *Modern Painting*.

———•◆•———

FORM IN A WORK of art depends to a great extent on the best possible arrangement of the parts which make up the whole. The arrangement is the best when it is as pleasing as possible (to the eye and ear and feelings), as unified as possible (in the relation between the parts and the whole), and as meaningful as possible (in terms of the artist's purpose). Proportion, then, is the key to artistic structure. We have little difficulty in comprehending and judging the structure, or pattern, of a picture. We admire the picture's structure when the arrangement of parts is relative to the shape of the canvas; when there is a kind of balance, symmetrical or asymmetrical, within the outline; when the arrangement of details strikes us as being intrinsically right and suitable to the material; and when the whole thing seems to be put together according to some kind of plan, whether the plan be at once obvious or not. We judge the structure of a piece of sculpture or architecture on much the same grounds. Although music is, perhaps, more complicated than graphic or plastic art, even in this realm we learn to recognize form and to enjoy it. We can apply the criteria of aesthetic structure to the writer's work as well as to the painter's work; and in so doing we can look for and find, in the best literature, struc-

ture which is not unlike that of graphic art. This I think is a
legitimate activity of literary criticism.[1]

Hawthorne had a few ideas about structure, but on the
whole his knowledge of art theory was slight. In *The Marble
Faun* he compares a story to a tapestry, "woven with the best
of the artist's skill and cunningly arranged with a view to the
harmonious exhibition of its colors." In *The Blithedale Romance* he speaks of the effectiveness of "arrangement, of
picturesque disposition, and artistically contrasted light and
shade." We shall have more to say of color and of light-and-
shade in a later chapter. For the present we are interested in
Hawthorne's awareness of arrangement, or pattern, or structure. In the note-books he comments on some old statues of
Castor and Pollux which are badly stained: "but the glory of
form overcomes all these defects of color." [xxi, 203] He discusses the composition of Michelangelo's "Transfiguration"
and finds it not all it might be.[2] Hawthorne is certainly aware
of composition, although he is ignorant of its laws—in spite
of the fact that he puts them into practice with so much effectiveness. He is particularly aware of proportion in architecture, and in the note-books frequently has something to
say about it. He finds the spire of Salisbury Cathedral "of
such admirable proportion that it does not seem gigantic."
[xx, 170] The towers of Petersburg Cathedral "are massive,
but low in proportion to their bulk." [xx, 333] Santa Maria
degl' Angeli, at Rome, has no pretensions to "architectural
merit of any kind, or to any architecture whatever." [xxi,
224] And of the Cathedral of Florence, he notes that "there is

---

[1] "Form in the painter's sense has passed into the vocabulary of the modern
literary critic and is used by him to designate the total aesthetic organization of a
piece of writing, the particular mold within the typical mold, so that a novel may
be spoken of as poorly conceived and lacking in form though it is clearly enough
a novel."—Gorham B. Munson, *Style and Form in American Prose* (New York,
Doubleday, Doran and Co., 1929), p. 18.

[2] "As regards the composition of the picture, I am not convinced of the propriety
of its being in two so distinctly separate parts,—the upper portion not thinking of
the lower, and the lower portion not being aware of the higher." (1858) [xxi,
341-42]

far more breadth and freedom of interior, in proportion to the actual space, than is usual in churches." [xxii, 48] He is surprised by the "art and contrivance" at Stonehenge and at the "regular and even somewhat intricate plan." [xx, 178] York Minster lacks the plan which Hawthorne thinks it should have.[3] A church at Perugia is "neither Gothic nor classic, but a mixture of both, and most likely barbarous." [xxii, 10] There can be no doubt that Hawthorne has some taste, however undeveloped, and some feeling for style as well as for unity.

Although many of Hawthorne's works are rather formal in their structure, many of them are very loose. He evidently has a slight preference for informal organization. He prefers Gothic to classic and neo-classic architecture and sculpture, as we can see from the note-books. He describes a statue of Pope Benedict XII, "a fair Gothic monument," and says that he likes the "overflow and gratuity of device, with which Gothic sculpture works out its design," [xxii, 13] particularly after having seen so much classic art. This preference is apparent in what he says and in what he does not say in the note-books as well as in the general style of most of his writing. Nevertheless, he does use a formal, almost classic, structure in some of his tales, and in the note-books he seems to admire with a kind of awe tryptichs and the three-part clerestory windows which he saw in so many cathedrals.

One of the elements which contributes to structure is balance. Hawthorne has a fine sense of balance, and he exercises it both within single images and throughout the over-all structure of a story. Balance does not imply absolute symmetry. A passage from *The House of the Seven Gables* illustrates a balance which is perfect without complete repetition:

---

[3] "It stands in the midst of a small open space,—or a space that looks small in comparison with the vast bulk of the cathedral. I was not so much impressed by its exterior as I have usually been by Gothic buildings, because it is rectangular in its general outline and in its towers, and seems to lack the complexity and mysterious plan which perplexes and wonder-strikes me in most cathedrals." [xx, 149]

The Italian turned a crank; and, behold! every one of these small individuals started into the most curious vivacity. The cobbler wrought upon a shoe; the blacksmith hammered his iron; the soldier waved his glittering blade; the lady raised a tiny breeze with her fan; the jolly toper swigged lustily at his bottle; a scholar opened his book with eager thirst for knowledge, and turned his head to and fro along the page; the milkmaid energetically drained her cow; and the miser counted gold into his strong-box,—all at the same turning of a crank. Yes; and, moved by the selfsame impulse, a lover saluted his mistress on her lips! Possibly, some cynic, at once merry and bitter, had desired to signify, in this pantomimic scene, that we mortals, whatever our business or amusement,—however serious, however trifling,—all dance to one identical tune, and, in spite of our ridiculous activity, bring nothing finally to pass. For the most remarkable aspect of the affair was, that, at the cessation of the music, everybody was petrified at once, from the most extravagant life into a dead torpor. Neither was the cobbler's shoe finished, nor the blacksmith's iron shaped out; nor was there a drop less of brandy in the toper's bottle, nor a drop more of milk in the milkmaid's pail, nor one additional coin in the miser's strong-box, nor was the scholar a page deeper in his book. All were precisely in the same condition as before they made themselves so ridiculous by their haste to toil, to enjoy, to accumulate gold, and to become wise. Saddest of all, moreover, the lover was none the happier for the maiden's granted kiss! [VII, 235-36]

Hawthorne presents all the figures in the first part of the description, but he leaves out two of them in the last part. For the sake of an implied symmetry, he begins each list with the cobbler and blacksmith, and ends them with the lover; he then rearranges the other figures according to another plan. This is a method often used by painters and sculptors. We shall see later how Hawthorne likes to balance the parts of a story, sometimes quite mathematically, sometimes asymmetrically.

The structure of a story can be balanced in many different ways, and occasionally two or more structures are used within a single tale. The two-part pattern is not common in Hawthorne, nor is it as effective as other plans. It is used in "My Kinsman, Major Molineux" and, as one of two methods, in *The Blithedale Romance*. Though a two-part story can be perfectly balanced, the story tends to fall apart in the middle. The three-part plan, as we saw it in "The Maypole of Merry Mount," is, I believe, the most common in Hawthorne. This pattern has clarity and simplicity which make it a favorite with painters, musicians, and architects, as well as story-writers. Four parts are not convenient, and I know of no successful attempt to use this form in Hawthorne's works. "The Great Stone Face" is a fine example of the five-part structure. "Fancy's Show-Box" seems to be in six parts, within a frame, but actually it is a variation on the three-part form. Some of Hawthorne's most complex, and successful, stories are in seven parts. "The Artist of the Beautiful," to be discussed in a chapter of its own, is a splendid example of this. Like most of the seven-part stories, it has four major parts separated by three minor parts. A large group of Hawthorne's tales and sketches, which I like to think of as frieze-stories,[4] may have any number of parts—often it is seven. Some of these stories are mere parades, such as "The Procession of Life," "A Select Party," "A Virtuoso's Collection," and some of them are sequences, or sketches, such as "Monsieur du Miroir," "A Rill from the Town Pump," or "The Toll-Gatherer's Day." There are a dozen more, but none of them is a completely developed story with sufficient artistic merit to justify our consideration.

It must not be thought for a moment that the present study is an attempt to prove that *all* Hawthorne's stories and novels

---

[4] F. O. Matthiessen says of these frieze-stories: ". . . in them Hawthorne was trying to encompass the range of society by presenting a procession of types, grouped together not by the external accidents of their trades or professions, but by their hidden desires or their deeper bond of suffering. These sketches, for the most part hardly more than notes for undeveloped themes, at least show how he was feeling his way from the short story toward the wider scope of the novel, which he already thought, during these years at the Manse, would alone justify his continuing to write." *American Renaissance* (New York, Oxford University Press, 1941), p. 239.

are equally good, even from the standpoint of design, color
imagery, rhythm, structure, and the other elements of art
with which we are dealing. Many of his works, like some of
the frieze-stories, have very little artistic worth. Some of them
have interesting rhythmic motifs, but are lacking in form;
some may have good over-all structure, but are devoid of any
line, mass, or color worth mentioning. This much can be said
for Hawthorne, however: when a story has a structure that
is aesthetically notable, it usually has some of the other
characteristics of all good art. Despite an irregularity in the
matter of structure, many of Hawthorne's tales repay consideration from this point of view.

Seldom does he leave the organization of his material to
chance. When he seems to do so, that very characteristic often
constitutes the pattern. Most of the time the reader is not
aware of the story's structure—it is so well hidden. But the
plan is there and its presence leaves the reader with the feeling that the story or sketch is indeed a work of art. We are
often not conscious of what it is that lends the artistic quality
until we examine the story carefully. In "Howe's Masquerade," for example, the structure is felt but is not apparent at
first. When we look closely we find an arrangement which is
based, like that of "The Maypole of Merry Mount," on a
particular distribution of imagery. Here is a story that consists essentially of a parade of figures. (It is one of the better
frieze-stories.) There is the framing that appears so often in
Hawthorne, in this case the visit of the author to the Province
House and the elderly gentleman's narrative. A typical pic-
ture-frame story! The incident within the frame, divided into
three parts, is a spectacle for the entertainment of Sir William Howe's guests.

A number of costumed figures parade down the great
staircase and out of the house. But Hawthorne is not content
merely to march the figures without order. True, the order
is chronological. Hawthorne is not satisfied with this, because
a chronological order alone would not be artistic. There is

selection and composition. To see this, we must look carefully at three or four passages in the story. After the funereal
music has begun and the master-of-ceremonies has opened
the doors, the first group of figures appears:

> The foremost was a man of stern visage, wearing a steeple-
> crowned hat and a skull-cap beneath it; a dark cloak, and
> huge wrinkled boots that came halfway up his legs. Under
> his arm was a rolled-up banner, which seemed to be the
> banner of England, but strangely rent and torn; he had a
> sword in his right hand, and grasped a Bible in his left. The
> next figure was of milder aspect, yet full of dignity, wearing
> a broad ruff, over which descended a beard, a gown of
> wrought velvet, and a doublet and hose of black satin. He
> carried a roll of manuscript in his hand. Close behind these
> two came a young man of very striking countenance and
> demeanor, with deep thought and contemplation on his
> brow, and perhaps a flash of enthusiasm in his eye. His
> garb, like that of his predecessors, was of an antique fashion,
> and there was a stain of blood upon his ruff. In the same
> group with these were three or four others, all men of
> dignity and evident command, and bearing themselves like
> personages who were accustomed to the gaze of the multi-
> tude. [II, 12-13]

Dark, sober, harsh is the picture of men in this first group.
Except for the third man who had "perhaps a flash of enthusiasm in his eye" and a "stain of blood upon his ruff,"
there is no color and little sparkle in this description. The
stain of blood adds the touch of color which Hawthorne
rarely fails to include.

After a few comments by the observers and Colonel Joliffe's
identifications, the second group appears:

> The first was a venerable and white-bearded patriarch, who
> cautiously felt his way downward with a staff. Treading
> hastily behind him, and stretching forth his gauntleted hand
> as if to grasp the old man's shoulder, came a tall, soldier-
> like figure, equipped with a plumed cap of steel, a bright
> breastplate, and a long sword, which rattled against the
> stairs. Next was seen a stout man, dressed in rich and courtly
> attire, but not of courtly demeanor; his gait had the swing-

ing motion of a seaman's walk; and chancing to stumble
on the staircase, he suddenly grew wrathful and was heard
to mutter an oath. He was followed by a noble-looking
personage in a curled wig, such as are represented in the
portraits of Queen Anne's time and earlier; and the breast
of his coat was decorated with an embroidered star. While
advancing to the door, he bowed to the right hand and to
the left, in a very gracious and insinuating style; but as he
crossed the threshold, unlike the early Puritan governors,
he seemed to wring his hands with sorrow. [II, 15]

The difference between these two descriptions is great. Here
there is life and vibrancy: "plumed cap of steel, a bright
breastplate, and a long sword" (there was a sword in the first
description, too, but it had no sparkle), "rich and courtly
attire," "Queen Anne's time," and the "gracious and insinuating style." There is movement in the old man's cautious de-
scent, the hasty treading of the second figure, "the swinging
motion of a seaman's walk," and the wringing of the hands.
There is even sound in this paragraph: the sword, the oath,
and the tapping of the old man's staff.

Now let us look at the third group:

The one in advance had a thoughtful, anxious, and somewhat crafty expression of face, and in spite of his loftiness
of manner, which was evidently the result both of an
ambitious spirit and of long continuance in high stations,
he seemed not incapable of cringing to a greater than himself. A few steps behind came an officer in a scarlet and
embroidered uniform, cut in a fashion old enough to have
been worn by the Duke of Marlborough. His nose had a
rubicund tinge, which, together with the twinkle of his eye,
might have marked him as a lover of the winecup and good
fellowship; notwithstanding which tokens he appeared ill
at ease, and often glanced around him as if apprehensive of
some secret mischief. Next came a portly gentleman, wearing
a coat of shaggy cloth, lined with silken velvet; he had
sense, shrewdness, and humor in his face, and a folio
volume under his arm; but his aspect was that of a man
vexed and tormented beyond all patience, and harassed almost to death. He went hastily down, and was followed by
a dignified person, dressed in a purple velvet suit, with very

rich embroidery; his demeanor would have possessed much
stateliness, only that a grievous fit of the gout compelled him
to hobble from stair to stair, with contortions of face and
body. [II, 16-17]

It is scarcely necessary to point out the differences between
this passage and the first or second one. This one has color,
more detailed movement, and characterization which is subjective as well as objective.

The light grows dim and another group passes down the
staircase, although Hawthorne does not describe these figures
in any detail. Finally a solitary man appears, the last of the
procession:

> A figure had come into view as if descending the stairs;
> although so dusky was the region whence it emerged, some
> of the spectators fancied that they had seen this human
> shape suddenly moulding itself amid the gloom. Downward
> the figure came, with a stately and martial tread, and reach-
> ing the lowest stair was observed to be a tall man, booted
> and wrapped in a military cloak, which was drawn up
> around the face so as to meet the flapped brim of a laced
> hat. The features, therefore, were completely hidden. But
> the British officers deemed that they had seen that military
> cloak before, and even recognized the frayed embroidery
> on the collar, as well as the gilded scabbard of a sword
> which protruded from the folds of the cloak, and glittered
> in a vivid gleam of light. . . . The martial shape again drew
> the cloak about his features and passed on; but reaching the
> threshold, with his back towards the spectators, he was seen
> to stamp his foot and shake his clenched hands in the air.
> [II, 20-22]

The pattern which Hawthorne follows leads him from flat,
colorless, more-or-less lifeless generalization to rounded, colorful, lively, characterizing description; then he varies the
scheme by presenting a group with practically no description;
and finally, and here his real artistry shows up, he shows us
a single figure which, while pictured in some detail, is sombre
and foreboding and rather vague, the more so because the
author has established a pattern which led us to expect even

greater brilliance and vitality. It might be argued, of course, and with some validity, that the earlier governors of the colony were less colorful men, that their clothes were dull and sombre, and that therefore Hawthorne is only being historically accurate when he pictures the men in the first group in dark, plain shades, with little action and brilliance. But he could have made them more colorful and brilliant if he had chosen to do so.[5] It is probable that Hawthorne deliberately chose to paint the earlier figures at Howe's masquerade in quiet, sombre tones—in order to carry out his pattern. The series of descriptions are too well arranged to admit chance. The structure of the story is clear, but not obvious.

It was stated above that the three-part structure is a favorite with Hawthorne. This is the form which he has given to "The Hollow of the Three Hills." In this story we see two women, one "graceful in form and fair of features," and the other "withered, shrunken, and decrepit." Behind them we see the impressive background:

> Three little hills stood near each other, and down in the midst of them sunk a hollow basin, almost mathematically circular, two or three hundred feet in breadth, and of such depth that a stately cedar might but just be visible above the sides. Dwarf pines were numerous upon the hills, and partly fringed the outer verge of the intermediate hollow, within which there was nothing but the brown grass of October, and here and there a tree-trunk that had fallen long ago, and lay mouldering, with no green successor from its roots. One of these masses of decaying wood, formerly a majestic oak, rested close beside a pool of green and sluggish water

---

[5] Endicott, the first of the figures in the first group, is pictured here as darker and more stern than any of the others. In "Endicott and the Red Cross," however, Hawthorne said of him: ". . . a man of stern and resolute countenance, the effect of which was heightened by a grizzled beard that swept the upper portion of his breastplate. This piece of armor was so highly polished that the whole surrounding scene had its image in the glittering steel." [II, 277] "The Gray Champion" pictures a man who might have been Endicott, and in any case was a figure from Endicott's time. He is portrayed as old and very gray, but none the less energetic, active, and vital.

at the bottom of the basin. Such scenes as this (so gray tradition tells) were once the resort of the Power of Evil and his plighted subjects; and here, at midnight or on the dim verge of evening, they were said to stand round the mantling pool, disturbing its putrid waters in the performance of an impious baptismal rite. The chill beauty of an autumnal sunset was now gilding the three hill-tops, whence a paler tint stole down their sides into the hollow. [1, 269-70]

The whole story is a carefully composed picture in every detail. Within its frame, the story falls into three parts, the three visions of the young woman. The entire composition is dominated by the three hills which are mentioned a half dozen times during the six pages. After the opening description, Hawthorne speaks of "the hollow depth between the three hills," "the hollow between three hills," "those three lonely hills," and finally the "Hollow between three Hills." This repetition is not only a rhythmic motif running through the story, but it is also a closely-knit part of the total composition which supports the tripartite design. So strong is this unit of three, that we tend to read in a kind of three-stress rhythm, and we are surprised to find so many sentences in the story which easily fall into three parts. That the author had a three-part symmetry in mind seems obvious. He mentions the three little hills six times; he makes the basin which the hills form "almost mathematically circular"; he gives the young woman three visions. The composition of this story reminds us of Grant Wood's picture, "American Gothic"—in structure only. Mr. Wood pictures two figures against a background which is built up around a motif of three. The man's shirt shows three stripes of three lines each; there are three tines on his pitch-fork; the construction of his overalls repeats this design; there are three seams on each of the tin roofs; there are two groups of three trees each; and even the potted plants on the porch repeat the motif of three. In the painting there are more details to support the dominant design than in Hawthorne's story, but the three-part design is certainly present.

"Fancy's Show-Box" also reminds us of a painting, but in a different way. It is like the "Maids of Honor" by Velasquez —a picture of the painting of a picture—only done by Hogarth, whom Hawthorne admired so much. Or it is like a Rembrandt self-portrait, where we see the painter holding his brush and looking at his picture of himself. Or it is like a Renaissance altar-piece, a series of pictures on the same subject within a single frame. Or, perhaps more accurately, in spirit at least, it is like an early twentieth-century expressionist painting by Chagall or Kandinsky, where a man is portrayed not realistically but by means of the objectification of his thoughts. "Fancy's Show-Box," in spite of Hawthorne's label, "A Morality," is a portrait, a study of Mr. Smith. We see Mr. Smith looki g at himself in a glass of Madeira. We see the six views that he sees: three of them are what really happened, those shown by Memory; and three of them, the ones presented by Fancy, picture the crimes which were projected but never perpetrated. Thus this story is indeed a kind of expressionist painting. The details are real, the objects recognizable, but it is an interpretative portrait rather than a representative one. The frame of the portrait is Hawthorne's discussion of guilt. It is an elaborate bit of carving, and it makes us ask ourselves, as so many elaborate frames do: does the frame exist for the picture or the picture for the frame? Within this frame is the three-part pattern, with two sections to each part.

We find this three-part structure in several other short tales. "Egotism; or, the Bosom-Serpent" is one of this type. It is rather unusual in that to the thread of the story, parts one and three, comparatively little space is given. The first part (about thirteen per cent of the total) deals with Elliston's first and unsuccessful visit to Roderick. The second part (about sixty-five per cent of the whole) is a kind of flashback. Elliston wants to learn more about Roderick before he calls on him again, and his findings make up this second and middle section. The third part (about twenty-two per

cent) shows us the second visit and the denouement. Hawthorne is not always algebraic in the structural balance of his
stories, but there is frequently a simple balance as there is
here.

Roughly the same proportions appear in "The White Old
Maid." The middle part, which is about half the length of
the whole story, is separated from the first part by the
haughty woman's exit from the house and from the last part
by her entrance again thirty or forty years later. The first
and the last of the three sections present action which occurs
within the house; the action of the middle section takes place
elsewhere. The Negro servant looked at the old maid "with
an ugly expression of merriment" just before she left the
house. Just after she reentered, having been admitted by "the
very image" of this same servant, one of the onlookers ex-
claimed, "such a hideous grin . . . was never seen on the face
of mortal man, black or white." This repetition is an element
in the story's symmetrical balance. The symmetry is made
almost perfect by imagery which is nearly identical at the
beginning and end of the story. On the first page we read:

> The moonbeams came through two deep and narrow
> windows, and showed a spacious chamber richly furnished
> in an antique fashion. From one lattice the shadow of the
> diamond panes was thrown upon the floor; the ghostly light,
> through the other, slept upon a bed, falling between the
> heavy silken curtains, and illuminating the face of a young
> man. . . .
> Suddenly, the fixed features seemed to move, with dark
> emotion. Strange fantasy! It was but the shadow of the
> fringed curtain waving betwixt the dead face and the moon-
> light, as the door of the chamber opened . . . [II, 186]

At the end of the story, on the last page, a similar scene is
presented:

> He snatched the torch from his companion's hand, and
> threw open the door with such sudden violence that the
> flame was extinguished, leaving them no other light than
> the moonbeams, which fell through two windows into the

spacious chamber. . . . As the priest and layman advanced
into the chamber, the Old Maid's features assumed such a
semblance of shifting expression that they trusted to hear the
whole mystery explained by a single word. But it was only
the shadow of a tattered curtain waving betwixt the dead
face and the moonlight. [II, 202]

The three-part pattern lends itself, perhaps more than other
forms, to symmetrical balance. "Ethan Brand," too, is divided into three parts, but they are of almost equal length.
The first part Hawthorne uses to fill in the background—
both exposition and setting—and to introduce all of the principal characters. The second part might be thought of as an
interlude, although it is related to the other two parts functionally. This section is devoted largely to descriptions of
Ethan's old friends, the German Jew with his diorama, and
the little dog's antics; it advances the plot very little; but it
does serve to give variety to the general tone of the whole
story. The third part is the big scene where Ethan tends the
fire and finally casts himself into the lime-kiln.

According to his wife's testimony, Hawthorne felt that the
structure of "The Great Stone Face" was too mechanical.[6]
Hawthorne, she reported, did not think the story was all that
it should be as a work of art. It is true, of course, that the
structure of this story is mechanical and rather obvious, but
not a great deal more so than that of Hawthorne's other tales.
In spite of its obviousness and simplicity, the plan of "The
Great Stone Face" is one of the best we shall find. The story
consists of five structural parts. Each of the first four parts
has the same general pattern. The first section gets the action
started and just before its end Ernest expresses the hope that
he may live to see the man who will look like the stone face:
"His mother was an affectionate and thoughtful woman,
and felt that it was wisest not to discourage the generous
hopes of her little boy. So she only said to him, 'Perhaps you

---

[6] From a letter to her mother (1849), quoted in Julian Hawthorne, *Nathaniel
Hawthorne and his Wife* (Boston, James R. Osgood and Co., 1884), I, 354.

may.'" [III, 33] Hawthorne then goes on to describe the influence of the face on Ernest's life and to indicate his kindly and intelligent character. The second part deals with the arrival of Mr. Gathergold. At its conclusion, we find a repetition of the pattern established at the end of part one. This time, however, the assurance comes from the Great Stone Face itself: "'He will come! Fear not, Ernest; the man will come!'" [III, 39] We then learn something of the development of Ernest's character and personality. Part three treats of General Blood-and-Thunder's arrival. It concludes with the same note of hope: "'Fear not, Ernest,' said his heart, even as if the Great Face were whispering him,—'fear not, Ernest; he will come.'" [III, 46] This is followed by further comment on the breadth of Ernest's wisdom and the depth of his kindness. In the fourth section, Hawthorne describes the arrival of Old Stony Phiz. The pattern is again repeated when the stone face seems to say, "'Fear not; the man will come!'" [III, 52] and when the author once more describes Ernest's expanding development. The fifth and last part of the story repeats the pattern of parts two, three, and four to the extent of bringing in another character who, Ernest hopes, may be the image of the stone face. Hawthorne varies the treatment of this figure, the poet, as well as the conclusion of the section. As we know, Ernest himself is "the man." The middle three sections are identical in form. The ending of the first section follows the pattern as does the beginning of the fifth section. Thus the story's structure is balanced without depriving the tale of a normal opening and closing.

"David Swan" has a structure which is so simple it is scarcely worthy of the name. It, too, falls into five parts: the beginning and end, which are a kind of frame, but too much a part of the whole to be separated, and the middle three parts. Each of the middle parts recounts one of the adventures which the sleeping David did not have. Hawthorne arranges these adventures in just the right order: wealth, love, death—from impermanence to permanence, perhaps. The middle one, in which the author uses no dialogue, is the shortest, and it is also the most vivid. Vibrant movement is provided in this section by the dancing movements of the girl and the flashing and buzzing of the bee. There is also a touch of color in the girl's deep blushes. Furthermore, this second part offers David wealth and success as well as love: had David wakened and met the girl, his future would have been brighter than that offered by Wealth or Death. The very simplicity of structure in this tale strengthens its meaning.

The structure of "Rappaccini's Daughter" is made up of seven parts. The first, third, fifth, and seventh are major sections and carry the main action of the story. The second, fourth, and sixth are minor parts, and here the action tends to stand still. A brief survey of the story will reveal the nature of this seven-part plan. In part one, Hawthorne sets the stage and introduces the characters. Giovanni sees Beatrice and begins to feel her influence. Part two, the first minor section, describes Giovanni's visit to Signor Baglioni. Here we learn a little about the work which Rappaccini and his daughter are doing, and the Baglioni-Rappaccini rivalry is indicated. Part three shows Giovanni's first meeting with Beatrice and further describes her unaccountable power. In the fourth part, the second minor section, Giovanni meets Baglioni on the street. We learn more of Rappaccini's wizardry and of the risk which Giovanni is taking, as well as Baglioni's desire to foil Rappaccini. Part five takes Giovanni into the garden. Part one showed to him the garden and Beatrice; part two introduced him to Beatrice; and now part five throws him headlong into the garden and subjects him directly to Beatrice's influence. Part six, which is the third and the last of the minor sections, brings Baglioni to Giovanni's room. The whole story is echoed in Baglioni's tale of the Indian princess. The warning is repeated and, to strengthen it, Giovanni is given an antidote for the poison. This is the first stage of Baglioni's plan to destroy Rappaccini's work. In part seven, Giovanni realizes that he, too, has been cursed with a poisonous breath. He faces Beatrice with his knowledge, and suggests that they do whatever they can to throw off the horror. Beatrice drinks the antidote and dies as a result.

This story has a neat structure. The major parts show the increasing influence of Rappaccini's garden and narrate the details which keep the story rolling along to its outcome. The minor parts deal with Giovanni's relationship to Signor Baglioni. These minor sections do something else of interest: they gradually draw Baglioni into the principal stream of the story. Beatrice's death is the direct result of Baglioni's antidote and is his means of destroying Rappaccini's scientific experiment. Baglioni's appearance at the end of the story and his question, which is the final line, " 'And is *this* the upshot of your experiment?' " completes the interweaving of the two separate threads.

The seven-part pattern is so complicated that, despite its effectiveness, we are not surprised to find so few examples of it. "The Christmas Banquet" has seven parts, but it has a frame around it—Roderick's presentation of his manuscript. Within the frame we find the seven parts divided into major and minor sections. Parts one, three, five, and seven carry the main drift of the story and keep it moving. Parts two, four, and six are descriptive lists of the guests; the action stops at these points. "The Artist of the Beautiful," as we shall see later, has seven parts, and, according to one of its two schemes, *The House of the Seven Gables* falls into seven parts. But this pattern is necessarily rare, particularly in fiction as short as some of Hawthorne's stories.

"My Kinsman, Major Molineux" has a structure which is different from that of the other stories. It is a weak plan in that it falls into two almost exactly equal parts. It is strong, however, in the way in which Hawthorne has joined the two parts together. In the first half of the story, Robin wanders around the town and finally arrives at the point at which the second half of the story occurs. The second half is like a scene in the center of an involved spiral. We have to ignore the difference between spatial and temporal design to view it this way, but the resulting clarity of the pattern justifies the process. In the first part of the story, Robin has met various people, most of whom turn up again in part two. In this way, as well as by the spiral design, Hawthorne has joined together the two parts of the story and has strengthened an otherwise weak structure.

There have been several references to the *frame* of a story. This is a device which Hawthorne often uses. Picture frames serve several purposes: they define the limits of the composition; they are decorative and, if completely adequate, the decoration contributes to the color, line, and general style of the picture; they keep the picture intact, prevent its collapsing in a rumpled heap, and enable us to hang it on the wall. The frame of a story does the same thing. It controls the spread of the incident: the story cannot exceed the limits established by its frame. The frame adds color to the story— this means interest; and the character of the frame can emphasize certain elements within the story itself. At the same time, the frame gives body to the incident; many an incident, particularly in Hawthorne where the incidents are often very slight, would be left in space if it were not for the surrounding structure. Hawthorne wrote at a time when picture-frames were elaborate, heavy, gilded affairs. Today we tend to criticize such frames, but they often served their purpose well. Imagine a portrait by Peale or a historical panorama by Cole or Trumbull. The picture, in a massive, gilded, rococo frame, is hanging in an early nineteenth-century drawing-room or gallery. The illumination is gaslight or possibly candle-light. The flickering flame changes the light reflected from the gilt frame and makes the frame, too, flicker and vibrate. This tremulous light blends perfectly with the surroundings and with the content and form of the picture within the frame. The same picture, in one of our modern simple frames would lose much of its charm. So, too, would a Cézanne at the Museum of Modern Art lose much if it were mounted in a foot-wide and foot-thick gilded frame. Modern frames are less heavy and in some ways less decorative than older ones, but if they are really good they can contribute something to the picture. Often they have a touch of color which helps to bring out the colors in the picture, either by contrast or by repetition. The width of the frame, the space between frame and picture, the contour of the moulding—all these things, even in modern pictures and frames, are a part of the total impression made on the mind of the observer.

A writer has some advantages over a painter in this matter of frames. Many painters, particularly the older ones, made their own frames; but many of them have very little control over the manner in which their pictures will be mounted. Writers, however, are more fortunate. They can write their frames and attach them permanently to their stories. They can thus be assured that the frame will not only suit the story but will actually enhance it, as some of Hawthorne's do.

Let us look at what he has done with "Dr. Heidegger's Experiment." The tale itself, the actual picture (which is the experiment), begins when the four subjects drink the magic liquid. It ends when they dolefully cry: " 'Are we grown so old again, so soon!' " Before the experiment begins, there are one hundred and eighty lines, nearly half of the whole. In these paragraphs the stage is set, the properties are arranged, and the mood is established. They are not simply part of an introduction, however, because they are part of a frame which surrounds the entire story. The conclusion, seventeen lines, is the rest of the frame. It is here that Hawthorne points the moral. This frame forces the story to remain within limits: the story deals only with the experiment, not with what went before or what followed in the lives of the characters. It sets the spirit of the story by stressing the fantastic and curious aspect of Dr. Heidegger as well as of the room in which the experiment is to take place.[7] And it keeps an otherwise very slim incident from flying off into space. One more thing may be said regarding the frame of this story. It is not a frame in the sense that it simply motivates or explains the narration of a story, as the frames in the "Legends of the Province House" do. The material which surrounds Dr. Heidegger's strange experiment is narrative and is a part of the whole.

What of the picture within the frame? If we shift our attitude and now think of it as something temporal rather than spatial, we shall see its compact and unusual pattern. With the liberty we are taking throughout this study, we can view the account of the experiment as, perhaps, a piece of music, something progressing through time. Like the Ravel "Bolero," the narration of the experiment builds in intensity. The "Bolero" depends for its increase in tension not so much on a stepping-up of tempo as on an increase in the number of instruments, on a changing in the quality of instruments, and on a rising pitch level. Hawthorne's pattern in this story immediately suggests musical structure. Let us allow our imaginations to roam and think of this as music. When the guests take their first drink of the magic water, there is a single melody, low and calm. As the drink begins to work on them, the melody becomes slightly more involved, but it is still single and low. With the second drink the music becomes more intense and the melody begins to break up into two, and then three, and finally four strains, an elaborate counterpoint—as the four subjects react in four different

---

[7] It is interesting to note that Poe, in "The Philosophy of Composition," uses the word *frame* in relation to the setting of a story or poem. The *locale*, he says, "has the force of a frame to a picture. It has an indisputable moral power in keeping concentrated the attention, and, of course, must not be confounded with mere unity of place."—F. C. Prescott (ed.), *Selections from the Critical Writings of Edgar Allan Poe* (New York, Henry Holt and Co., 1909), pp. 161-162.

While thinking of Poe and of "Dr. Heidegger's Experiment," we should remember that Poe said of this story: "The artist breathes in every line of it."—*Ibid.*, p. 98.

ways. The third drink introduces a change in tempo, perhaps waltz time. The counterpoint shifts to the simple cords of the waltz. The music becomes more and more intense, breaking into six-eight time, and the simple cords fly off in all directions and defy all laws of musical composition—as the gentlemen quarrel over the lady. The pitch becomes higher, the notes more rapid and irregular, and finally it all resolves into a strong, high discord—as the vase with the magic water breaks. Underneath all this there has been a low, rumbling, monotonous, and somewhat unrelated bass, Dr. Heidegger. When the water is spilled the bass booms out. Suddenly the entire pattern of notes reverses itself. Whereas perhaps fifty measures were used to build up to the crash, the reversal, down to the beginning again, takes ten measures—as the young people rapidly become old again. " 'Are we grown so old again, so soon!' cried they, dolefully." The original melody, now in a minor key, is heard once more, and the composition is ended.

Criticism of this kind is impressionistic, to say the least. I think it calls attention, however, to the emotional impact of this story, while at the same time it points out the unusual structure on which Hawthorne has built his account of the experiment. It is doubtful whether Hawthorne knew much about music. It is improbable that he thought of "Dr. Heidegger's Experiment" in terms of music. But there is no doubt in my mind that he intended the story to have just the emotional effect which the musical pattern suggests. Regardless of his ignorance of musical form, his sense of artistic form in general is great enough to enable him to create a story according to a musical pattern. I have expressed the structure of this tale in terms of musical composition simply to illustrate the vitality and variety of Hawthorne's aesthetic imagination. Basically this story is built on a five-part pattern; but it is much more than that. It is so free and expansive that the formal division into five parts seems scarcely worth mentioning.

To try to fit as complex a novel as *The House of the Seven Gables* into a rigid pattern is absurd, and it is more absurd to talk about this book in terms of numbers. However, the facts are that *The House of the Seven Gables* does fit a pattern, and the number *seven* seems to be more than casually significant. There are seven principal characters: Hepzibah, Clifford, Jaffray, Phoebe, Holgrave, Uncle Venner, and Ned Wiggins. (If we want to push matters a bit, we can count seven characters from the past who wield a strong influence over the present: the original Maule, the builder Maule, the carpenter Maule; Alice; Colonel Pyncheon, the store-keeper Pyncheon, and Gervayse Pyncheon.) The twenty-one chapters of the novel can be divided structurally into three parts of seven chapters each. Part A opens with the historical background; introduces Hepzibah, Holgrave, Uncle Venner, and Ned; brings in Phoebe; gives us a mere glimpse of Jaffray; and brings in Clifford. Part B opens with Jaffray's appearance and his offer to help take care of Clifford; shows the care given Clifford, and his recuperation; includes Holgrave's narrative of the hypnotism of Alice; and concludes with Phoebe's departure. Part C opens with Jaffray (as part B did) and his demands to see Clifford; narrates the death of Jaffray; describes the flight of Hepzibah and Clifford; pictures the dead Jaffray; brings back Phoebe; winds up the love-story; brings Hepzibah and Clifford back; and rounds off the whole story in conclusion. We find that part A is essentially introductory; part B is a quiet middle section; and part C is the intense final section with the three most exciting chapters in the book, "Clifford's Chamber," "The Flight of Two Owls," and "Governor Pyncheon."

If we divide the twenty-one chapters into seven groups of three, we find that each group has its own function in the story. The first group is introductory and presents the permanent residents of Pyncheon Street: Hepzibah, Holgrave, and the gingerbread-eating Ned. The second group of three chapters deals principally with Phoebe and her arrival. The third group is devoted chiefly to Clifford. The fourth, and middle, group is static and descriptive, being concerned with daily life in the house. The fifth group, after the interlude of chapter twelve which is Holgrave's story of Alice, deals with Phoebe's departure. The sixth group includes the intense activity of chapters sixteen, seventeen, and eighteen, mentioned above: this group is really the climax of the story. The seventh, and last, group describes Phoebe's return and unties the knots. This seven-fold division is less tight and less significant than the better organized three-part division, but its presence justifies mentioning it. Interlaced, as it is, through the three parts of the novel, it undoubtedly helps to tie it all together.

Thus we can see that there is a flow and balance to the structure of *Seven Gables*. It has a beginning, a middle, and an end, and these parts are not only quantitatively balanced but they are also, we might say, qualitatively balanced. They are functionally as well as structurally equal. Henry James has pointed out that *Seven Gables* "is not so rounded and complete as *The Scarlet Letter*." [8] This is probably true. Hawthorne may have thought it a better novel than the earlier one, but from our standpoint it is weaker. Nevertheless, it has structure—an elaborate pattern—and from this point of view, at least, it is artistically conceived.

Even *The Blithedale Romance* has an element of balance in its structure, and there are three structural devices worth noticing. The book is divided neatly into two parts by the middle chapter, chapter fifteen, which the author calls "The Crisis." It is in this chapter that Coverdale and Hollingsworth part company. Coverdale's refusal to cooperate with Hollingsworth is a true turning-point in the story: it is the first step in the collapse of the community and it is the first great blow to Hollingsworth. Up to this point the affairs of the four characters have sailed along on a comparatively unruffled sea. From here on difficulties are many. Thus, chapter

---

[8] *Hawthorne* (New York, Harper and Brothers, 1879), p. 119.

fifteen makes an artistic division in the composition. There are, in addition, two other devices which tend to illuminate the pattern of this novel. Professor Westervelt first appears in chapters eleven and twelve. His next major appearance is in chapters twenty-two and twenty-three (although he has entered the picture briefly in chapters eighteen and twenty). In other words, Westervelt's influence was first *felt* about a third of the way through the novel and then *seen* at about the two-thirds mark. The remaining method of balancing the story is potentially an excellent one, but it falls short of perfection. Hawthorne opens the romance with old Moodie, and the first chapter is largely concerned with him. Chapter ten, which shows his appearance on the farm, and chapter twenty-two, which narrates his story, are nicely spaced, breaking the book into three approximately equal parts. If Hawthorne had brought Moodie into his last chapter, as he very well might have, instead of writing the ridiculous and meaningless confession, *The Blithedale Romance* would have had an artistic and significant structure. Of course, the broad scope of any novel is its own apology for the lack of obvious over-all form.

The less said about the structure of *The Marble Faun* the better! It is not a well organized novel. It is balanced only arbitrarily: the two books are of equal length. The whole story can be thought of as having three parts, however unequal in length: the first twenty-three chapters (nearly all of Book One) deal more or less with all of the four principal characters; the next twelve chapters (up to about half-way through Book Two) deal chiefly with Kenyon and Donatello; the last fifteen chapters, principally with Hilda and Kenyon. Each of these parts has its own high point: the murder of the model in part one; the reconciliation of Donatello and Miriam in part two; and the reunion of Kenyon and Hilda in part three. It looks as if Hawthorne had a fairly good plan for this novel but did not follow it. These three parts are very unequal in length, and when we discount for the numerous interludes which are unrelated to the action of the story—particularly in Book Two—the parts become even more dissimilar in length. Briefly, the novel lacks structure. It is too long, too rambling, and has too many disconnected though very charming irrelevancies. In form it is not a good novel: in content—though this is not the province of our study—its awkwardness is obvious. Why Hawthorne's last completed novel, written when he presumably knew most about art, should be the weakest artistically I do not know. Perhaps this is a problem for the biographer. The fact remains. Hawthorne's after-thought, which he labeled "Conclusion," is his own confession of the story's weakness.

3. Design

"The most obvious and easily distinguishable pure forms which painting employs are line, mass, colour relations, from which are occasioned motion, pattern, and rhythm, and their accessories balance and thrust."—RHYS CARPENTER, *The Aesthetic Basis of Greek Art.*

———————●•●———————

WHEN WE LOOK critically at a picture, we can see how the painter has used the various elements of design. We note line in the painting, for example, and observe how certain lines seem to dominate, how the points of interest in the picture are stressed by lines which focus our attention on them, how the painter has suggested movement or stability by means of lines which seem to move or to remain fixed. We notice also the use and effectiveness of mass. We look for the relationships between masses in the total composition of the picture, and the means by which the artist has developed masses—color, light-and-dark, or form. We look for rhythm. And finally, we look for contrast. Contrasting colors, lines, masses, and movements are, perhaps, as important as rhythm. Certainly the two together are as important to form in art as significance is to content.

The analogy between plastic or graphic art and prose writing is difficult to explain and to illustrate. But when we bear in mind that our purpose is not to look at Hawthorne's writings simply as literary compositions, but as examples of art comparable to other art-products (remembering the point of view established in the opening chapter of this study), we can *see* these elements of design in his writing just as we can in a painting or a statue. We shall see many interesting examples of Hawthorne's use of artistic design.

He had very little theoretical knowledge of design as he had very little theoretical knowledge of structure in art. During the years he spent traveling and looking at pictures and statues, he developed some feeling for design, and occasionally he made rather acute critical comments. After his visit to the Durham Cathedral, in 1857, his note-book entry indicated a critical reaction, which was probably intuitive, but which reflects considerable taste and feeling.[1] His interest in the technical aspects of sculpture, the art most immediately concerned with mass, was never very great. Throughout the note-books his discussions of sculpture consist largely of comments on broken noses and on questions of taste and morals relative to undraped statues. He admired the rough texture of Powers' works, and in some of his talks with Powers he appears to have a faint conception, however crude and vague, of the purpose of sculpture. In *The Marble Faun,* of course, sculpture is important and much talked about. But there is very little said about the technical aspects, and nowhere does Hawthorne's interest go beyond a naive concern with content. He has even less technical and critical understanding of line, although in his practice he uses line effectively. Of rhythm and contrast he has nothing to say that would suggest a theoretical knowledge. However, he

---

[1] "The pillars of the nave are immensely thick, but hardly of proportionate height, and they support the round Norman arch; nor is there, as far as I remember, a single pointed arch in the cathedral. The effect is to give the edifice an air of heavy grandeur. It seems to have been built before the best style of church architecture had established itself; so that it weighs upon the soul, instead of helping it to aspire. First, there are these round arches, supported by gigantic columns; then, immediately above, another row of round arches, behind which is the usual gallery that runs, as it were, in the thickness of the wall, around the nave of the cathedral; then, above all, another row of round arches, inclosing the windows of the clere-story. The great pillars are ornamented in various ways,— some with a great spiral groove running from bottom to top; others with two spirals, ascending in different directions, so as to cross over one another; some are fluted or channelled straight up and down; some are wrought with cheverons, like those on the sleeve of a police inspector. There are zigzag cuttings and carvings, which I do not know how to name scientifically, round the arches of the doors and windows; but nothing that seems to have flowered out spontaneously, as natural incidents of a grand and beautiful design." [XXI, 8-9]

uses these elements constantly and with a great deal of artistry.

It is strange that mass, the design element about which Hawthorne seems to know the most (judging from his interest in architecture), is the one used least in his writings. It is probably much more difficult for a writer to achieve mass, either two- or three-dimensional, than to achieve color or even line. Hawthorne sometimes creates a sense of mass through sheer bulk and weight, as in the following sentences from *The Marble Faun:*

> Their road wound onward among the hills, which rose steep and lofty from the scanty level space that lay between them. They continually thrust their great bulks before the wayfarers, as if grimly resolute to forbid their passage, or closed abruptly behind them, when they still dared to proceed. A gigantic hill would set its foot right down before them, and only at the last moment, would grudgingly withdraw it, just far enough to let them creep towards another obstacle. Adown these rough heights were visible the dry tracks of many a mountain torrent that had lived a life too fierce and passionate to be a long one. Or, perhaps, a stream was yet hurrying shyly along the edge of a far wider bed of pebbles and shelving rock than it seemed to need, though not too wide for the swollen rage of which this shy rivulet was capable. A stone bridge bestrode it, the ponderous arches of which were upheld and rendered indestructible by the weight of the very stones that threatened to crush them down. Old Roman toil was perceptible in the foundations of that massive bridge; the first weight that it ever bore was that of an army of the Republic.
>
> Threading these defiles, they would arrive at some immemorial city, crowning the high summit of a hill with its cathedral, its many churches, and public edifices, all of Gothic architecture. . . . A thousand years, at all events, would seem but a middle age for these structures. They are built of such huge, square stones, that their appearance of ponderous durability distresses the beholder with the idea that they can never fall,—never crumble away,—never be less fit than now for human habitation. [x, 127-29]

A strong feeling of solidity and mass pervades this passage. Size, height, weight, and even anger and old age contribute to the massiveness of these hills, the bridge, and the buildings. Hawthorne has given bulk to the whole picture without depriving any of its parts of their normal proportion.

When he attempts plasticity (which is mass in three dimensions), he sometimes relies on light to help him get the effect he wants.[2] One short passage from "Edward Fane's Rosebud" will illustrate this sculpture-like quality:

> The blaze quivers capriciously in front, alternately glimmering into the deepest chasms of her wrinkled visage, and then permitting a ghostly dimness to mar the outlines of her venerable figure. [II, 318]

Despite Hawthorne's comparative ignorance of the technique and aesthetic of sculpture, a feeling for plastic treatment is evidenced in his first description of the Great Stone Face. When we read the following paragraph, we can *feel* the solidity and shape of the figure:

> The Great Stone Face, then, was a work of Nature in her mood of majestic playfulness, formed on the perpendicular side of a mountain by some immense rocks, which had been thrown together in such a position as, when viewed at the proper distance, precisely to resemble the features of the human countenance. It seemed as if an enormous giant, or a Titan, had sculptured his own likeness on the precipice. There was the broad arch of the forehead, a hundred feet in height; the nose, with its long bridge; and the vast lips, which, if they could have spoken would have rolled their thunder accents from one end of the valley to

---

[2] In his note-books, Hawthorne reports (1858) a discussion with Powers regarding a Michelangelo statue. This discussion occurred after Hawthorne had completed most of his works. "I asked Powers what he thought of Michelangelo's statue of Lorenzo de' Medici. He allowed that its effect was very grand and mysterious; but added that it owed this to a trick,—the effect being produced by the arrangement of the hood, as he called it, or helmet, which throws the upper part of the face into shadow. The niche in which it sits has, I suppose, its part to perform in throwing a still deeper shadow. It is very possible that Michelangelo may have calculated upon this effect of sombre shadow, and legitimately, I think . . ." [XXII, 120]

the other. True it is, that if the spectator approached too near, he lost the outline of the gigantic visage, and could discern only a heap of ponderous and gigantic rocks, piled in chaotic ruin one upon another. Retracing his steps, however, the wondrous features would again be seen; and the further he withdrew from them, the more like a human face, with all its original divinity intact, did they appear; until, as it grew dim in the distance, with the clouds and glorified vapor of the mountains clustering about it, The Great Stone Face seemed positively to be alive. [III, 30-31]

While Hawthorne was writing this passage, he must have been alertly conscious of the idea that sculpture is design in space. He sets his figure in space and emphasizes this by letting us move very close to the face and then farther and farther away from it. In that manner we see it in space and we also sense its plastic nature. Furthermore, the author has carved his figure with large and simple details: a forehead, a nose, and lips—much as Borglum has carved his figures in the Black Hills.

As a sculptor, Hawthorne does not do as well with Drowne's wooden image. He paints her gaudily (though this is really not Hawthorne's doings, but Drowne's: Hawthorne knows better) and he fails to give her the space she needs. To his credit, however, it must be said that he does not use too many details, at least in the face:

> . . . intelligence and sensibility brightened through the features, with all the effect of light gleaming forth from within the solid oak. The face became alive. It was a beautiful, though not precisely regular, and somewhat haughty aspect, but with a certain piquancy about the eyes and mouth which, of all expressions, would have seemed the most impossible to throw over a wooden countenance. [V, 97]

The rest of the figure, with its laced bodice, draped petticoat, flowered hat, fan, earrings, watch, and all the other small details, is much too minutely carved—particularly for the use to which this wooden image was to be put. By contrast, the Great Stone Face is all the more competent sculpture. The larger the figure, in sculpture, the fewer the details: Hawthorne apparently knew, or at least sensed, this axiom. In any case, he handled the large face with skill.

Turning to Hawthorne's use of line, we find many more and varied illustrations. He is a fairly adequate draughtsman and he uses line for many purposes. His sense of line used as an aid to focusing attention is shown in a statement from "The Lily's Quest." Lily and Adam have been followed, while they look for a suitable place to build their "temple of Happiness," by the gloomy figure of Gascoigne. They turn and look at him.

> The old man stood just behind them, so as to form the chief figure in the group, with his sable cloak muffling the lower part of his visage, and his sombre hat overshadowing his brows. [II, 296]

The author not only has skill enough to group his figures in a triangle, with Gascoigne at the apex, but he also knows, evidently, that such an arrangement will make the old man "the chief figure in the group." In *The Blithedale Romance,* Hawthorne repeats the direction and shape of a line and thus gives emphasis to it:

> It was a spectacle to behold how, with a tumbler in each hand, he tossed the contents from one to the other. Never conveying it awry, nor spilling the least drop, he compelled the frothy liquor, as it seemed to me, to spout forth from one glass and descend into the other in a great parabolic curve, as well defined and calculable as a planet's orbit. He had a good forehead, with a particularly large development just above the eyebrows . . . [VIII, 251]

The curve of the eyebrow repeats the parabolic curve made by the bartender's liquor. In the note-books, where this bartender first appears, there is no reference to the eyebrows,[3] and consequently the picture loses much of its charm.

---

[3] "Chiefly, they drank plain liquors, gin, brandy, or whisky, sometimes a Tom and Jerry, a gin cocktail (which the bartender makes artistically, tossing it in a large parabola from one tumbler to another, until fit for drinking), a brandy smash, and numerous other concoctions." [XVIII, 476]

Hawthorne's draughtsmanship shows to good advantage in some of his descriptions of buildings. By means of a few well-placed lines, he is able to establish definite architectural designs. Mr. Gathergold's house in "The Great Stone Face" is a good example of this:

> It had a richly ornamented portico, supported by tall pillars, beneath which was a lofty door, studded with silver knobs, and made of a kind of variegated wood that had been brought from beyond the sea. The windows, from the floor to the ceiling of each stately apartment, were composed, respectively, of but one enormous pane of glass . . . [III, 36]

When we add to this a preceding comment, "the exterior was of marble, so dazzlingly white," which is a matter of mass and color, we get a fairly good picture of the house. This building can be compared with a house in "My Kinsman, Major Molineux."

> It was a large, square mansion, distinguished from its neighbors by a balcony, which rested on tall pillars, and by an elaborate Gothic window, communicating therewith. [III, 312]

Or another house, that of Roderick Elliston in "Egotism; or the Bosom-Serpent":

> It was a large, sombre edifice of wood, with pilasters and a balcony, and was divided from one of the principal streets by a terrace of three elevations, which was ascended by successive flights of stone steps. [v, 50]

A variety of lines moving in all directions makes up the picture of the old mansion in *The House of the Seven Gables:*

> There it rose, a little withdrawn from the line of the street, but in pride, not modesty. Its whole visible exterior was ornamented with quaint figures, conceived in the grotesqueness of a Gothic fancy, and drawn or stamped in the glittering plaster, composed of lime, pebbles, and bits of glass, with which the woodwork of the walls was overspread. On every side the seven gables pointed sharply towards the sky, and presented the aspect of a whole sisterhood of edifices, breath-

ing through the spiracles of one great chimney. The many lattices, with their small, diamond-shaped panes, admitted the sunlight into hall and chamber, while, nevertheless, the second story, projecting far over the base, and itself retiring beneath the third, threw a shadowy and thoughtful gloom into the lower rooms. Carved globes of wood were affixed under the jutting stories. Little spiral rods of iron beautified each of the seven peaks. On the triangular portion of the gable, that fronted next the street, was a dial, put up that very morning, and on which the sun was still marking the passage of the first bright hour in a history that was not destined to be all so bright. All around were scattered shavings, chips, shingles, and broken halves of bricks; these, together with the lately turned earth, on which the grass had not begun to grow, contributed to the impression of strangeness and novelty proper to a house that had yet its place to make among men's daily interests. [VII, 10-12]

Curved lines, straight lines, circles, and triangles make this picture a notable line-drawing. To avoid letting the eye run off the paper, Hawthorne twice draws it back again by turning the lines inward to the interior of the house. At the end of the description, to give balance and stability to the drawing, he lowers our glance to the "lately turned earth" and the grass which "had not begun to grow." Another picture, drawn with diagonal lines, is seen in *Seven Gables:*

At a little distance stood a wooden church, black with age, and in a dismal state of ruin and decay, with broken windows, a great rift through the main body of the edifice, and a rafter dangling from the top of the square tower. Farther off was a farm-house, in the old style, as venerably black as the church, with a roof sloping downward from the three-story peak, to within a man's height of the ground. It seemed uninhabited. There were the relics of a wood-pile, indeed, near the door, but with grass sprouting up among the chips and scattered logs. The small rain-drops came down aslant; the wind was not turbulent, but sullen, and full of chilly moisture. [VII, 387-88]

Again Hawthorne keeps the centre of attention within the picture and gives the whole a firm foundation. The broken windows, the great rift, the dangling rafter, the sloping roof, and the slantwise rain are all drawn on the angle. The square tower and the upward movement of the grass furnish artistic contrasts. We cannot fail to note that both these passages from *Seven Gables* are devoid of color. They are drawn in black and white, with perhaps a gray wash here and there.

By means of lines a feeling of movement (sometimes empathic) can be aroused. Once movement is introduced, a third dimension can often be seen and felt. In another passage from *Seven Gables* Hawthorne does this:

> The sunshine might now be seen stealing down the front of the opposite house from the windows of which came a reflected gleam, struggling through the boughs of the elm-tree, and enlightening the interior of the shop more distinctly than heretofore. The town appeared to be waking up. A baker's cart had already rattled through the street, chasing away the latest vestige of night's sanctity with the jingle-jangle of its dissonant bells. A milkman was distributing the contents of his cans from door to door; and the harsh peal of a fisherman's conch-shell was heard far off, around the corner. [VII, 54]

The reader's eye, aided later by his ear, is carried in a linear movement down, in, out, across, and finally "around the corner."

There is a remarkable use of line in "The Ambitious Guest." By direct and implied movement, Hawthorne takes the reader's eye upward, downward, or across, and often lets it pause for a moment. An interesting thing about line and movement is that certain kinds of lines suggest movement, and certain kinds of movement suggest line. In painting, the artist cannot actually paint movement: he has to rely on line (and rhythm) to suggest it. In writing, however, the artist can work it both ways. He can suggest lines so arranged that they in turn will suggest movement; or he can describe movements which will establish line. (For the sake of simplicity, I shall use the term *line* regardless of whether line is the cause or the effect.) Hawthorne uses both of these

methods. A phrase such as this one suggests upward movement followed by downward movement: "a mountain
towered above their heads, so steep, that the stones would
often rumble down its sides." A transverse movement followed by a restful pause is felt in the passage: "a wagon
rattled along the road, and stopped a moment before the
door." In both of these examples the two methods are at
work. The phrase "a mountain towered above their heads"
might be an example of line which suggests movement;
while "the stones would often rumble down its sides" is
movement which suggests line. The two methods working
together give the best results, and in many of these illustrations from "The Ambitious Guest" we shall see this double
device at work.

The first two sentences in the story show lines moving in
all directions:

> One September night, a family had gathered around their
> hearth, and piled it high with the drift-wood of mountain
> streams, the dry cones of the pine, and the splintered ruins
> of great trees that had come crashing down the precipice.
> Up the chimney roared the fire, and brightened the room
> with its broad blaze. [II, 121]

This is an example of Hawthorne's building a line pattern
by direct movement. Here is one which we might call the
result of implied movement:

> He was of a proud, yet gentle spirit—haughty and re-
> served among the rich and great; but ever ready to stoop his
> head to the lowly cottage door, and be like a brother or a
> son at the poor man's fireside. [II, 124-25]

The downward line in the phrase "to stoop his head to the
lowly cottage door" seems to attribute an upward thrust
to "haughty and reserved among the rich and great." Of
course, in any story where there is movement there is certain to be line. The whole pattern of "The Ambitious Guest"
is one of upward and downward-moving lines relieved by
transverse lines and pauses. This design element is certainly

more prominent here than in most of Hawthorne's stories. We find many such upward-moving lines as "the whole family rose up," "spring forward to meet them" (a diagonal), "high and abstracting ambition," "came up at nightfall from the valley," "noble pedestal for a man's statue," "flame arose," and the charming one at the end of the story, "light smoke was seen stealing from the cottage chimney, up the mountain-side." Downward-moving lines are, naturally, more frequent in this tale. We find such examples as "rushing down the steep side of the mountain," "tumbles over the precipice," "downcast smile," and the one downward-moving line for which all the other lines in the story exist, "The slide! The slide!" followed by "down came the whole side of the mountain in a cataract of ruin." Transverse lines support and emphasize these up-and-down lines. There are, for example, "passed through the Notch," "along the road," "rushed from their cottage," and even such implied ones as "passed over the daughter's spirit" and "resounded in broken notes between the cliffs." Many more lines of each type could be listed, but they lose their force when taken from the con-- text. We have seen enough to realize that line is the dominant design element in "The Ambitious Guest" and that the story offers vivid illustrations of this device.

Line and movement are presented in Hawthorne's description of the Fountain of Trevi, in *The Marble Faun:*

> At the foot of the palatial façade was strewn, with careful art and ordered irregularity, a broad and broken heap of massive rock, looking as if it might have lain there since the deluge. Over a central precipice fell the water, in a semicircular cascade; and from a hundred crevices, on all sides, snowy jets gushed up, and streams spouted out of the mouths and nostrils of stone monsters, and fell in glistening drops; while other rivulets, that had run wild, came leaping from one rude step to another, over stones that were mossy, slimy, and green with sedge, because, in a century of their wild play, Nature had adopted the Fountain of Trevi, with all its elaborate devices, for her own. Finally, the water tumbling, sparkling, and dashing, with joyous haste and never-ceasing

murmur, poured itself into a great marble-brimmed reservoir, and filled it with quivering tide; on which was seen, continually, a snowy semicircle of momentary foam from the principal cascade, as well as a multitude of snow-points, from smaller jets. The basin occupied the whole breadth of the piazza, whence flights of steps descended to its border. [IX, 199-200]

By lines always pointing downward and by an occasional contrasting horizontal line, the author pictures a downward movement. It is one of the best examples of his use of line. We can compare this with another passage, from a few pages farther on in the novel, in which the movement is upward:

... a red twinkle of light was visible amid the breadth of shadow that fell across the upper part of the Coliseum. Now it glimmered through a line of arches, or through a broader gleam as it rose out of some profound abyss of ruin; now it was muffled by a heap of shrubbery which had adventurously clambered to that dizzy height; and so the red light kept ascending to loftier and loftier ranges of the structure, until it stood like a star where the blue sky rested against the Coliseum's topmost wall. [IX, 215]

In the first of these two passages Hawthorne has developed his movement by continuous downward-moving lines; in the second, not by continuous line at all but by spots of light, separate from each other, but unified, through the very movement they create, into an upward-moving diagonal line. In *The Blithedale Romance,* we find another example of upward movement. By careful manipulation of lines, Hawthorne leads our glance up and up:

Late in the afternoon, the weathercock on the church spire indicated a change of wind; the sun shone dimly out, as if the golden wine of its beams were mingled half-and-half with water. Nevertheless, they kindled up the whole range of edifices, threw a glow over the windows, glistened on the wet roofs, and, slowly withdrawing upward, perched upon the chimney-tops; thence they took a higher flight, and lingered an instant on the tip of the spire, making it the final point of a more cheerful light in the whole sombre scene. [VIII, 230]

Then, with his feeling for contrast and his fine sense of balance and finality (to be discussed more fully at the end of this chapter), he brings the eye down to earth again, literally and figuratively:

> The next moment, it was all gone. The twilight fell into the area like a shower of dusky snow; and before it was quite dark, the gong of the hotel summoned me to tea. [VIII, 230]

The nocturnal wanderings of Robin, in "My Kinsman, Major Molineux," constitute a line drawing which has surprising design and continuity. The pattern which these lines form resembles a kind of square spiral (mentioned in the discussion of structure) or perhaps one unit in an elaborate Roman-key design, in which, after many turnings, the line arrives at a point within the centre of the formation. Robin entered the town and roamed about looking for his uncle.

> He now became entangled in a succession of crooked and narrow streets, which crossed each other, and meandered at no great distance from the water-side. . . . But the streets were empty, the shops were closed, and lights were visible only in the second stories of a few dwelling-houses. At length, on the corner of a narrow lane, through which he was passing, he beheld the broad countenance of a British hero swinging before the door of an inn, whence proceeded the voices of many guests. [III, 298]

Following his experience in the inn, he proceeded to his search for Major Molineux.

> On turning the corner of a narrow lane, Robin found himself in a spacious street, with an unbroken line of lofty houses on each side, and a steepled building at the upper end, whence the ringing of a bell announced the hour of nine. . . . At length, after many pauses to examine the gorgeous display of goods in the shop-windows, and after suffering some rebukes for the impertinence of his scrutiny into people's faces, the Major's kinsman found himself near the steepled building, still unsuccessful in his search. As yet, however, he had seen only one side of the thronged street; so Robin crossed, and continued the same sort of inquisition down the opposite pavement . . . [III, 303-304]

He turned another corner and ventured into a different section of the town and "entered a street of mean appearance on either side of which a row of ill-built houses was straggling towards the harbor." He is back again near the water-side. Here he has a rather narrow escape and hurries on.

> He now roamed desperately, and at random, through the town. . . . The streets lay before him, strange and desolate, and the lights were extinguished in almost every house . . . he was passing beneath the walls of a church which formed the corner of two streets, when, as he turned into the shade of its steeple, he encountered a bulky stranger, muffled in a cloak. [III, 308-309]

This is the man who finally tells him to stay where he is and wait for his uncle to pass by. Whether this church is the same one whose steeple Robin has seen twice before, we cannot tell. It may be; that, at least, is the impression we get. In any case, it is the picture's centre around which Robin's meandering has taken him. Hawthorne has drawn a zigzagy line which is centered around and eventually arrives at a specific point. At each turning of the line there is a bright spot. The line is sometimes narrow and sometimes wide, and, even where there are many people on the street, the line seems to be bleak and isolated, by virtue of Robin's discouragement and loneliness. Hawthorne has defined the line more sharply by describing the buildings on each side of the streets; and by picturing the bleakness and loneliness of the streets, he has emphasized the linear quality. In this instance, as in many examples cited throughout this study, the predominance of an image and the repetition by which it is built up argue for a definite plan in the mind of the author. Hawthorne must have intended to create this zigzag spiral effect. If he had not, it is doubtful whether he would have given so much stress to this kind of movement. The whole picture seems too well organized and balanced to admit chance.

An interesting diagonal line appears several times in

"Feathertop." It is a small detail, but it adds graphic vigor to the story. Dickon has lighted Mother Digby's pipe for the second time:

> She drew in a long whiff and puffed it forth again into the bar of morning sunshine which struggled through the one dusty pane of her cottage window. [IV, 317]

When the scarecrow learns to smoke, he too "at length blew forth a volley of smoke extending all the way from the obscure corner into the bar of sunshine." And again:

> . . . it applied itself lustily to the pipe, and sent forth such abundant volleys of tobacco smoke that the small cottage kitchen became all vaporous. The one sunbeam struggled mistily through, and could but imperfectly define the image of the cracked and dusty windowpane on the opposite wall. [IV, 322-23]

Three times Hawthorne introduces this diagonal line of sunlight as it filters through the smoke. He is trying a device which stage-designers use to bring out a shaft of light—smoke. And, for variety, he increases the density of the smoke each time. He does the same thing in two passages in *The Marble Faun:*

> . . . Hilda now looked up into the dome, where the sunshine came through the western windows, and threw across long shafts of light. . . . These great beams of radiance, traversing what seemed the empty space, were made visible in misty glory, by the holy cloud of incense, else unseen, which had risen into the middle dome. [x, 201]

A few pages later we find a similar account:

> Before leaving the church, they turned to admire again its mighty breadth, the remoteness of the glory behind the altar, and the effect of visionary splendor and magnificence imparted by the long bars of smoky sunshine, which travelled so far before arriving at a place of rest. [x, 222]

Again shafts of light create moving lines.[4]

---

[4] The suggestion for these last two passages is found in the note-books. "The great slanting beam of sunshine was visible all the way down to the pavement,

Movement can be suggested through line in such a way that the means, the use of line, is not readily apparent. When we examine a piece of austere architecture such as the Cathedral of Siena or the Parthenon, for example, or a modern building such as the Bronx County Courthouse, we find that the austerity and plainness of the façade is broken by lines which contribute vibrancy to the total image. The fluting of the columns, the metope sculptures, the frieze, the triglyphs, the string-courses, and the steps—such details as these lend variety and interest because they are motion set off against the more quiet masses of the larger unit. Occasionally, Hawthorne uses words and phrases which accomplish the same purpose for his stories as these architectural details do for buildings. In "The Minister's Black Veil" two motifs of this type run through the story. One of them is the use of words which suggest trembling: "the hearers quaked," "the corpse had slightly shuddered, rustling the shroud and muslin cap," "the people trembled," "the bride's cold fingers quivered in the tremulous hand of the bridegroom," "his frame shuddered," "they were made to quake," "his most convulsive struggles," "shivering with the arms of death around him," and others. The second device, though similar in purpose, is more specific and has a more drastic and vivid effect. It consists of a number of references to the trembling of the black veil: "it shook with his measured breath," "they longed for a breath of wind to blow aside the veil," "even the lawless wind . . . never blew aside the veil," and "his faint breath caused it to stir." These references, and some other synonyms of *vibrate,* are too frequent to be accidental. Hawthorne must have used them intentionally, and perhaps consciously, as he used spots of light in this story and others, and as architects use graven details to enliven as well as to decorate their work.

---

falling upon motes of dust or a thin smoke of incense imperceptible in the shadow. Insects were playing to and fro in the beam, high up toward the opening." [xxi, 352] It is interesting to note that in the finished product, the novel, Hawthorne leaves out the insects, as perhaps an inartistic detail.

The same kind of thing appears in "Rappaccini's Daughter," where the vibrancy is partly the result of the brilliant color in the story, and partly, of quivering and tremulous images, produced by means of lines in motion. The water of Rappaccini's fountain "continued to gush and sparkle in the sunbeams." Beatrice, with her "glistening ringlets," is often seen moving in and out of the picture through the marble portal. In one place she is described as wearing "a look of desolate separation shuddering at itself." The flowers "glowed in the air." The reptile which had been poisoned "contorted itself violently." The insect "lingered in the air and fluttered about her head," and when it died "its bright wings shivered." Giovanni turned quickly about "as if an inanimate thing should start into feverish life." He saw "rustling leaves with the broken sunshine glimmering among them." His "pulses had throbbed with feverish blood." "A faintness passed like a shadow over Giovanni, and flitted away." At another point, he "became sensible of a burning and tingling agony in his hand." The spider's web "vibrated with a tremor originating in the body of the small artisan," and finally the spider "made a convulsive grip with his limbs." A swarm of insects were seen "flitting through the air." After Beatrice had taken Baglioni's antidote, "Giovanni trembled. Beatrice shuddered very nervously." These and other phrases help to give to "Rappaccini's Daughter" a scintillating vibration that accounts for much of its impressive strength.

We turn now to contrast, one of the most important artistic devices and one upon which Hawthorne leans heavily and uses with success. Painters, sculptors, architects, musicians, poets—all artists—employ contrast. Leonardo used it, and so does Thomas Benton, but perhaps the painter who reminds us most of Hawthorne is El Greco. Beethoven and Wagner—romanticists like Hawthorne—produce sharp variations in intensity and color of sound. Byron is a notable example of the poet who builds up images by contrast. Hawthorne does the same thing in much the same way.

Contrasting movement is used with skill in a passage from "The Minister's Black Veil":

> Few could refrain from twisting their heads towards the door; many stood upright, and turned directly about; while several little boys clambered upon the seats, and came down again with a terrible racket. There was a general bustle, a rustling of the women's gowns and shuffling of the men's feet, greatly at variance with that hushed repose which should attend the entrance of the minister. But Mr. Hooper appeared not to notice the perturbation of his people. He entered with an almost noiseless step, bent his head mildly to the pews on each side, and bowed as he passed his oldest parishioner, a white-haired great-grandsire, who occupied an armchair in the centre of the aisle. It was strange to observe how slowly this venerable man became conscious of something singular in the appearance of his pastor. He seemed not fully to partake of the prevailing wonder, till Mr. Hooper had ascended the stairs, and showed himself in the pulpit, face to face with his congregation, except for the black veil. [1, 42-43]

There is a change of pace in this paragraph that cannot be overlooked. It is like the variation in tempo between the different sections of the Parthenon frieze: the violent action of a group of horsemen as against the slower movement of men on foot. Another instance of this variety appears in the same story. When a deputation of the church is sent to call on Mr. Hooper and inquire into the mystery of the veil, Hawthorne devotes a long paragraph, with no dialogue, to describing the immobility and inefficiency of the committee. He concludes it by writing:

> Thus they sat a considerable time, speechless, confused, and shrinking uneasily from Mr. Hooper's eye, which they felt to be fixed upon them with an invisible glance. Finally, the deputies returned abashed to their constituents, pronouncing the matter too weighty to be handled, except by a council of the churches, if, indeed, it might not require a general synod. [1, 51]

The whole paragraph is slow moving, the sentences are long, and the words tend to be referential. But when Elizabeth,

Mr. Hooper's betrothed, determines to penetrate his secret, the spirit of the writing is quite different. There is dialogue, action, feeling. Toward the end of the discussion Hawthorne writes:

> "Have patience with me, Elizabeth!" cried he passionately. "Do not desert me, though this veil must be between us here on earth. Be mine, and hereafter there shall be no veil over my face, no darkness between our souls! It is but a mortal veil—it is not for eternity! O! you know not how lonely I am, and how frightened, to be alone behind my black veil. Do not leave me in this miserable obscurity forever!"
>
> "Lift the veil but once, and look me in the face," said she.
>
> "Never! It cannot be!" replied Mr. Hooper.
>
> "Then, farewell!" said Elizabeth.
>
> She withdrew her arm from his grasp, and slowly departed, pausing at the door, to give one long, shuddering gaze, that seemed almost to penetrate the mystery of the black veil. But, even amid his grief, Mr. Hooper smiled to think that only a material emblem had separated him from happiness, though the horrors which it shadowed forth must be drawn darkly between the fondest of lovers. [1, 54-55]

Here the discussion moves more rapidly, the sentences are shorter, and the words tend to be emotive. The length of sentences may not be particularly important or indicative; but it is interesting to note that, by actual count, the first passage (the deputation's silent interview) contains sentences which average twenty-six words in length, with most of the sentences containing more than twenty-five words. The second passage (Elizabeth and Mr. Hooper) contains sentences which average seventeen words in length, with most of them containing less than sixteen words. While these figures prove very little, they do point out one of the means Hawthorne uses to enliven his writing. By various means, one of which may be variety in sentence length, he is able to procure a change of pace, a difference in tempo. He uses sentences, much as a painter uses brush-strokes, to get different emotional effects.

A passage in "The Birthmark" will be worth some attention. It shows one of the ways in which Hawthorne builds up images, and offers several good examples of contrast. The first two sentences of the passage set the scene and indicate the general mood:

> When Georgianna recovered consciousness she found herself breathing an atmosphere of penetrating fragrance, the gentle potency of which had recalled her from her deathlike faintness. The scene around her looked like enchantment. [IV, 58-59]

The "penetrating fragrance" combined with "gentle potency" results in a fragrance which, though we cannot actually smell it, impresses us with its subtlety and seems almost to have color. When Hawthorne tells us that this odor "had recalled her from her deathlike faintness," we attribute supernatural power to the fragrance. Thus, in one sentence, which is actually vague and almost abstruse, the author has stimulated our imaginations to produce an amazing and unnatural scent. He continues by stating: "The scene around her looked like enchantment." This completes the mysterious power of the odor and shifts our attention to the room, a more tangible physical entity. We attribute to the room some of the odor's intangible, vague qualities. The next sentence introduces an image which is both a contrast and a repetition:

> Aylmer had converted those smoky, dingy, sombre rooms, where he had spent his brightest years in recondite pursuits, into a series of beautiful apartments not unfit to be the secluded abode of a lovely woman. [IV, 59]

There is contrast offered by the "smoky, dingy, sombre rooms" and the "beautiful apartments." At the same time, these words help to reinforce the unearthly and enchanted nature of the converted room. The "series of beautiful apartments" is made more spacious and hence more beautiful and even more lonely by the word "series." Had Aylmer converted the space merely into beautiful apartments, the image would have lost some of its awe. As it stands, we can imagine

Georgianna wandering around, alone in a *series* of rooms. The word "secluded," of course, contributes to this idea; and the phrase "beautiful woman" has its own natural magic. We have a complex picture, now, built-up of several similar and contrasting suggestions. But Hawthorne goes on:

> The walls were hung with gorgeous curtains, which imparted the combination of grandeur and grace that no other species of adornment can achieve; and as they fell from the ceiling to the floor, their rich and ponderous folds, concealing all angles and straight lines, appeared to shut in the scene from infinite space. [IV, 59]

The "gorgeous curtains" add to the picture. A space surrounded by curtains has a magnificence and at the same time a soundlessness which is both impressive and depressive. "Grandeur and grace" is really a contrast in itself. The two words are not often thought of together, but when they are applied to a room completely draped in curtains they fit perfectly. The curtains, we are told, "fell from the ceiling to the floor," thus making the enclosure complete and adding to the enchantment. "Rich and ponderous folds" have an objective effect by themselves, and in combination with "grace" produce a lack of consistency which adds to the unnatural quality of the whole room. The "angles and straight lines" remind us again that the room was originally a laboratory where Aylmer indulged in his "recondite pursuits"; this term also adds a good note of contrast to the "grandeur and grace" and "rich and ponderous folds." The scene is "shut in . . . from infinite space," and the one idea contrasts with the other and repeats the effect of the curtains. The room has been decreased in size and made more depressive, while at the same time the "series of beautiful apartments" expands the whole group of rooms and contracts the one room. The contradictory elements of the imagery tend to augment the unnaturalness of the whole picture. To what extent Hawthorne was conscious of building up images by repetition and contrast, I do not know. It may be the result of unconscious artistry or it may be the result of careful planning. Whatever the process, he certainly does achieve powerful, and somewhat impressionistic, effects by this means.

We shall pause at this point to look briefly at some isolated examples of contrast. Hawthorne often contrasts light and dark, and thus joins hands with many distinguished graphic artists. Time after time he sets light against dark, as in *The Blithedale Romance* when Coverdale speaks of his "pleasant bachelor-parlor, sunny and shadowy," or in the following passage from "Rappaccini's Daughter":

> . . . he seated himself near the window, but within the shadow thrown by the depth of the wall, so that he could look down into the garden with little risk of being discovered. All beneath his eye was a solitude. The strange plants were basking in the sunshine . . . [IV, 140]

These we might call static contrasts. Often Hawthorne makes contrasts which depend on movement. Two or three examples will illustrate this:

> An elderly man, with his pretty daughter on his arm, was passing along the street, and emerged from the gloom of the cloudy evening into the light that fell across the pavement from the window of a small shop. ("The Artist of the Beautiful") [v, 289]

> Nor could the young bride any longer deny that a radiance was breaking through the mist, and changing its dim hue to a dusky red, which continually grew more vivid, as if brilliant particles were interfused with the gloom. ("The Great Carbuncle") [I, 215]

> A little speck of azure has widened in the western heavens; the sunbeams find a passage, and go rejoicing through the tempest; and on yonder darkest cloud, born, like hallowed hopes, of the glory of another world and the trouble and tears of this, brightens forth the Rainbow. ("Sights from a Steeple") [I, 268]

These last two passages are suggestive of El Greco, particularly in the vivid "Toledo." Sometimes the members of the contrast are separated from each other. This separation makes for a pleasing suddenness without impairing the force of the contrast. We can see this in a passage from *The Blithedale Romance:*

> . . . I looked back over a long slope of pasture land, and beheld them standing together, in the light of sunset, just on the spot where, according to the gossip of the Community, they meant to build their cottage. Priscilla, alone and forgotten, was lingering in the shadow of the wood. [viii, 181]

Here, in addition to the light and dark, we find a contrast between the two figures and the single figure, too. Occasionally Hawthorne uses an indirect contrast, applying the characteristics of one thing to another, as in *The House of the Seven Gables* where he says that "the smile was sunshine under a thunder cloud" or, still better, "she was by nature as hostile to mystery as the sunshine in a dark corner." Or he may build a contrast upon a time lapse, as in "Roger Malvin's Burial": "The early sunbeams hovered cheerfully upon the tree-tops beneath which two weary and wounded men had stretched their limbs the night before." [v, 133]

Hawthorne's writings abound in color and color contrasts. (Color will be discussed at length in chapter five.) The purple tone of Rappaccini's garden is sharpened by the presence of an orange-colored reptile. The many spots of red in "The Minister's Black Veil" are heightened by the use of a green spot at the close of the story. Frequent shades of blue, purple, and violet contrast brilliantly with the general golden tone of *The Marble Faun.*

The entire story of "The Ambitious Guest" has already been seen to be a contrast between upward and downward-moving lines. Sometimes Hawthorne balances height against depth as in the implied contrast in *The Marble Faun:* " 'Yet we met once, in the bowels of the earth; and, were we to part now, our fates would fling us together again in a desert, on a mountain-top, or whatever spot seemed safest'." [IX, 130] Or again: "In the black depths, the Faun had found a soul, and was struggling with it towards the light of heaven." Contrasting settings are used effectively in this novel: Hilda's tower and the catacombs; the castle of Monte Beni and the foot of the Tarpeian rock. There are also some contrasts in the volume and quality of sound. The sound-pattern of "Young Goodman Brown" (to be discussed later) illustrates this, as does a passage from *Seven Gables:*

> . . . a political procession, with hundreds of flaunting banners, and drums, fifes, clarions, and cymbals, reverberating between the rows of buildings, marched all through town, and trailed its length of trampling footsteps, and most infrequent uproar, past the ordinarily quiet House of the Seven Gables. [VII, 238]

Employing whatever means he can to achieve the result he wants, Hawthorne uses contrast for many different purposes. He can emphasize differences in detail by reminding the reader of previous descriptions. "The severe and homely simplicity of the apartment, with its naked walls and brick pavement, looked strange, accustomed as Georgianna had become to the fantastic elegance of her boudoir." ("The Birthmark") [IV, 68-69] Or, he can help to unify a story by means of contrast, as that between the opening and closing scenes of "Ethan Brand." At the beginning of the story the night is dark, blacker than most nights against the contrasting glow of the lime-kiln. When the story ends, the sun is shining cheerfully, "in the promise of the bright day that was hastening onward." Or he can reinforce characterization by contrasting characters: Phoebe and Hepzibah, Hilda and Miriam, Priscilla and Zenobia, to list just a few of the many pairs. Or he can simply paint vivid pictures by contrast, as Zenobia's death in *The Blithedale Romance:*

> Her wet garments swathed limbs of terrible inflexibility. She was the marble image of a death-agony. Her arms had

grown rigid in the act of struggling, and were bent before her with clenched hands; her knees, too, were bent, and—thank God for it!—in the attitude of prayer. Ah, that rigidity! It is impossible to bear the terror of it. It seemed,—I must needs impart so much of my own miserable idea,—it seemed as if her body must keep the same position in the coffin, and that her skeleton would keep it in the grave . . . [VIII, 336]

Zenobia, as Hawthorne well knew, might have been expected to have a more decorative posture in death. Coverdale explains it:

Being the woman that she was, could Zenobia have foreseen all these ugly circumstances of death,—how ill it would become her, . . . she would no more have committed the dreadful act than have exhibited herself to a public assembly in a badly fitting garment! Zenobia, I have often thought, was not quite simple in her death. She had seen pictures, I suppose, of drowned persons in lithe and graceful attitudes. [VIII, 338]

The stiff, angular, horrible form contrasts with the soft, graceful figure of Zenobia and the gay, exotic flowers which she always wore in her dark hair.

One of the most effective uses of contrast is to build up the intensity of a denouement with a sweeping crescendo and then let it down again with a kind of diminuendo. Hawthorne lifts us to lofty heights, and then gently helps us down again. He winds up the spring which produces a great crash, and then lets the sound fade out. At the end of "Young Goodman Brown," after the tremendous tension of the Black Mass and Goodman Brown's final outburst, Hawthorne lets him and the reader relax:

Hardly had he spoken when he found himself amid calm night and solitude, listening to the roar of the wind which died heavily away through the forest. He staggered against the rock, and felt it chill and damp; while a hanging twig, that had been all on fire, besprinkled his cheek with the coldest dew. [IV, 122-123]

The devastating tragedy in "Feathertop" is relieved by Mother Rigby's calm observations on life and her request for another coal for her pipe. The horror of Roderick's bosom-serpent is pushed away forever by Rosina's optimism. The mystery in "Drowne's Wooden Image" is never satisfactorily explained, but Drowne's quiet return to his other work brings the whole thing back to reality again. "Roger Malvin's Burial" ends calmly with a prayer. Hawthorne's reassuring aesthetic comment eases the pain caused by the destruction of Owen Warland's butterfly. The agony in "The Wedding Knell" is soothed by the bridegroom's clarity of mind:

> "Forgive; and be forgiven. Yes; it is evening with us now; and we have realized none of our morning dreams of happiness. But let us join our hands before the altar, as lovers whom adverse circumstances have separated through life, yet who meet again as they are leaving it, and find their earthly affection changed into something holy as religion. And what is Time to the married of Eternity?" [1, 38-39]

In "The Minister's Black Veil" Father Hooper's clear vision of the meaning of life sweetens the bitterness of his life and death. Even the strenuous psychoanalysis of "The Hollow of the Three Hills" is made more cheerful by the last line of the story: " 'Here has been a sweet hour's sport,' said the withered crone, chuckling to herself." The diminuendo of "Dr. Heidegger's Experiment" is, of course, an intrinsic part of the story. After the landslide in "The Ambitious Guest," all is calm again:

> The next morning, the light smoke was seen stealing from the cottage chimney up the mountain-side. Within, the fire was yet smoldering on the hearth, and the chairs in a circle round it, as if the inhabitants had but gone forth to view the devastation of the Slide, and would shortly return, to thank Heaven for their miraculous escape. [11, 134]

The futility of Peter Goldthwaite's search is mitigated in part by John Brown's generosity. The ravaging destruction

of Oberon's stories in "The Devil in Manuscript" is lessened
by his feeling that his "brain has set the town on fire!" In
"My Kinsman, Major Molineux" the furious rage of the
revelers with their grisly burden is suddenly wiped out and
the tension is lessened:

> When there was a momentary calm in that tempestuous
> sea of sound, the leader gave the sign, the procession re-
> sumed its march. On they went, like fiends that throng in
> mockery around some dead potentate, mighty no more, but
> majestic still in his agony. On they went, in counterfeited
> pomp, in senseless uproar, in frenzied merriment, trampling
> all on an old man's heart. On swept the tumult, and left a
> silent street behind. [III, 325]

With sudden contrast, Hawthorne shifts from dark to light,
from noise to quiet, from war to peace, from chaotic tension
to calm relaxation, from a high and strained pitch to one
which is low and pleasing.

4. Rhythm

"Art could be called the image of man if for no other reason than that both alike are characterized by one attribute overshadowing every other. This attribute is rhythm. The human organism is built upon a design that is in all important respects symmetrical; and his vital reflexes, including breathing and heartbeat, are chains of regularly repeated movements. . . . Correspondingly in the spatial arts rhythm appears as simultaneous order in the guise of symmetry, and in the temporal arts as an order of sequence through the regular recurrence of an element. Equally in a building, a statue, and a painting, and in literature and music, rhythmic repetition like that exhibited in the living organism would seem to be the very basis of aesthetic structure."
—HELEN HUSS PARKHURST, *Beauty*

R HYTHM IS UNDOUBTEDLY one of the basic elements in art. It is also one of the most characteristic elements in Hawthorne. I like the simple definition which says that rhythm is the more-or-less regular repetition of a motif. The repeated motifs which make up a rhythmic sequence, in literature, may be any of several. They may be lines, static or moving. (Rhythm, in fact, is a kind of movement itself, because when a motif is repeated several times it suggests a forward movement.) The repeated motifs may be words or phrases, or colors, or masses, or whole images, or even sounds or philosophic concepts. Rhythm can be used for its own sake, or it can be used to focus attention. A painter can call our attention to a certain part of his picture by repeating its colors or its shape in various details throughout the composition. This device, in Hawthorne, I have called *prefiguration*. An author has a wider range of rhythmic motifs from which to choose than any other artist, and Hawthorne takes full advantage of this range. Sometimes his rhythmic sequences are harder to recognize than at other times. But even though they are not at once apparent, their force is felt and Hawthorne's prose gains immeasurably by their frequent use. We are not concerned here with so-called prose-rhythm which is in some way related to the rhythm of poetry, although there is, often, a rhythm of this type in Hawthorne, as we shall occasionally observe, and it does heighten the artistic effect of his writing. The kind of rhythm which concerns us in this study is produced by a repetition of stimuli which evoke in the reader's mind a sequence of images. Or, to state it in other terms, we are not interested as much in the accented beats of the music as we are in the recurring use of melodies and chords.

The repetition of Roderick's complaint in "Egotism; or the Bosom-Serpent" is easily spotted. Four times in the first third of the story the man with the snake in his bosom cries out, " 'It gnaws me! It gnaws me!' " Then there is a long gap and finally, on the next to the last page, just before the snake is expelled, Roderick again cries out, " 'It gnaws me! It gnaws me!' " Though this device is neither a prefiguration nor, strictly speaking, a rhythmic motif (because of the way it is distributed), it is a repeated phrase which has an emotional value and which appears to be part of the total design. When we have heard Roderick cry out four times in such close succession, we look forward to another appearance of the outburst. Hawthorne does not fail us. Wisely and with apparent forethought, he uses the phrase only once more and he holds it until almost the end of the story.

Several fine rhythmic motifs run through *The House of the Seven Gables*. The most obvious one is the repeated use of the phrase which is the title of the book. Many times Hawthorne refers to the house as "The Pyncheon house," or "the old house," or "the seven gables," or "the mansion," or by any one of a number of other names, including "the desolate, decaying, gusty, rusty old house of the Pyncheon family." Many times, also, he calls it "the House of the Seven Gables" —full title with capital letters. The use of this term might,

of course, be only a means of varying references to the house
which must necessarily be mentioned often. I suspect it is
this in part; but I also believe that Hawthorne saw some
poetic and artistic value in repeating the title. The validity
of this belief is strengthened when we realize that the term
is used with diminishing frequency throughout the book.
It is used twenty times in the first third of the novel; twelve
times in the middle third; and six times in the last third.
Perhaps Hawthorne wanted to establish the term and its
meaning and then found it less and less necessary to repeat
it. As in *The Scarlet Letter,* where the author unifies the
whole by his last line, so in this book the last line—"she
floated heavenward from the House of the Seven Gables!"—
seems to wrap up the story in its title and make it a compact
unit. The most frequent use of the phrase is in the first
chapter, the historical background. Here Hawthorne repeats
his title nine times. Interestingly, the chapter which is the
next in the frequency of this phrase is the thirteenth, "Alice
Pyncheon," which is another flash-back. In his story of Alice,
Holgrave uses the phrase seven times. We can almost think
that Hawthorne wanted to take time out for reinforcing the
significance of his title. All these repetitions have something of the effect of a refrain, like Poe's "Nevermore,"
Cowper's "My Mary," Kipling's "Lest we forget," or Dray-
ton's "On thy banks . . ." They gather both meaning and
emotional content as they are repeated. By the time we read
the last few repetitions of "the House of the Seven Gables"
we see all the color and feel all the passion that it has acquired
in its previous uses.

On the first page of this novel appears a passage which is
almost poetry, so strong is the rhythm of its words and its
repeated devices: "The street is Pyncheon Street; the house
is the old Pyncheon House; and an elm-tree, of wide cir-
cumference, rooted before the door, is familiar to every town-
born child by the title of the Pyncheon Elm." [vii, 1] The
same devices are used in the second chapter when Hawthorne

is speaking of Hepzibah: "born, too, in Pyncheon Street, under the Pyncheon Elm, and in the Pyncheon House . . ." Again, in the third chapter, we find a repetition of this motif, although it is somewhat broken-up:

> "See here!" cried he; "what do you think of this? Trade seems to be looking up in Pyncheon Street!"
> "Well, well, this is a sight, to be sure!" exclaimed the other. "In the old Pyncheon House, and underneath the Pyncheon Elm!" [vii, 64]

The three terms do not appear so close together again in the course of the story, but whenever Hawthorne uses one of them, the reader cannot help seeing and hearing the other two. The tree is mentioned often in the book, and, as we would expect of Hawthorne, in the last paragraph. Another brief poetic passage is found in the chapter in which Hawthorne, the all-seeing and all-knowing author, talks to the body of Jaffray Pyncheon:

> Up, therefore, Judge Pyncheon, up! You have lost a day. But to-morrow will be here anon. Will you rise, betimes, and make the most of it? To-morrow! To-morrow! To-morrow! We, that are alive, may rise betimes to-morrow. As for him that has died to-day, his morrow will be the resurrection morn. [vii, 402]

A motif which appears in *Seven Gables* with almost rhythmic regularity is Hawthorne's use of Alice Pyncheon, her flowers, and her music. We read of her first in chapter one where "Alice's Posies" are described. The flowers appear again in chapter five, and it is here that we find the first reference to Alice's harpsichord. Hepzibah tells Phoebe about Alice later in this same chapter. In chapter nine, Hawthorne describes Hepzibah as thinking about playing the harpsichord but wisely reconsidering. Chapter thirteen, entitled "Alice Pyncheon," is Holgrave's fantastic tale of Alice and Matthew Maule's grandson. In this chapter we see the girl with her "certain gentle and cold stateliness" bewitched by the carpenter. In chapter fifteen we hear the harpsichord for the first time: Clifford is playing it, and Hepzibah "involuntarily thought of the ghostly harmonies, prelusive of death in the family, which were attributed to the legendary Alice." The figure of Alice is among the ghosts who examine the Colonel's portrait after Jaffray's death, in chapter eighteen. "Alice's Posies" is the title of chapter nineteen, the chapter in which Phoebe returns to Pyncheon Street. In chapter twenty, Clifford refers to the flowers in connection with the romance of Phoebe and Holgrave. And in the last chapter, in the last paragraph, we read that Uncle Venner, as he left the house,

> . . . seemed to hear a strain of music, and fancied that sweet Alice Pyncheon—after witnessing these deeds, this bygone woe and this present happiness, of her kindred mortals— had given one farewell touch of a spirit's joy upon her harpsichord, as she floated heavenward from the HOUSE OF THE SEVEN GABLES. [VII, 467]

In sharp contrast to the tragic sweetness of the Alice motif is the awful horror of the Maule's blood motif. This sequence is, in one sense, the backbone of the novel because upon Maule's curse hangs the entire story. Hawthorne keeps it in the foreground with all its gory brilliance. Within the first half-dozen pages the curse is planted. " 'God,' said the dying man, pointing his finger, with a ghastly look, at the undismayed countenance of his enemy,—'God will give him blood to drink!' " [VII, 6] The motif is repeated later when the Colonel's body is discovered. ". . . a voice spoke loudly among the guests, the tones of which were like those of old Matthew Maule, the executed wizard,—'God hath given him blood to drink!' " [VII, 17] Before this mysterious voice spoke out, Hawthorne notes that the friends who discovered the body of the colonel saw that "there was blood on his ruff." As the author discusses the events following the strange death, he calls attention to vague rumors which were circulating, rumors to the effect "that there were marks of fingers upon his throat, and the print of a bloody hand on his plaited ruff."

Once more, still in the first chapter, Hawthorne tells us that
whenever a Pyncheon ". . . did but gurgle in his throat, a
bystander would be likely enough to whisper, between jest
and earnest,—'He has Maule's blood to drink!'" [vii, 25]
At the beginning of the second part of the story, there is
another reference to the curse:

> She had heard of the anathema flung by Maule, the executed
> wizard, against Colonel Pyncheon and his posterity,—that
> God would give them blood to drink,—and likewise of the
> popular notion, that this miraculous blood might now and
> then be heard gurgling in their throats. [vii, 178]

(Phoebe, incidentally, thought that she could hear this very
gurgle in Jaffray's throat.) We pick up the sequence again
in chapter thirteen. In Holgrave's story, the carpenter Maule
is talking with Alice's father, and when the old man becomes
so angry that he cannot talk, he "could only make a gurgling
murmur in his throat." Maule, the grandson, points out, "'so,
so you have old Maule's blood to drink!'" The author reminds us indirectly of the curse in chapter fifteen when he
places Jaffray in the elbow-chair in which Colonel Pyncheon
died, the chair in which Jaffray, too, is to die. We noted
that in the first chapter Hawthorne linked the Colonel's
blood-stained ruff with the curse. Now, in chapter seventeen, he lets this association carry the burden of the motif.
Clifford speaks of an elderly man "'sitting in an oaken
elbow-chair, dead, stone-dead, with an ugly flow of blood
upon his shirt bosom!'" Later in this chapter Clifford again
mentions this man "'sitting in an arm-chair, with a blood-
stain on his shirt-bosom.'" (This man, as we know, is
Jaffray.) Hawthorne picks up the motif again, in chapter
eighteen, when he speaks of Judge Pyncheon who might
have "to show himself at a dinner-table with that crimson
stain upon his shirt-bosom." And then, in the summary of
the last chapter, the author talks about the murder of Judge
Pyncheon's uncle and "a bloody hand-print on the old man's
linen." This is a direct reflection of one of the earliest ap-

pearances of the motif. Hawthorne has spun a composite
sequence which has emotional value of its own and which
helps to tie the story together.

We could cite several more equally effective motifs and
trace them through *Seven Gables*. There is Maule's well
which makes its first appearance on the eighth page of the
novel and its final appearance on the last page. All in all,
there are a dozen references to the well—to remind us of the
general stagnation of the house in Pyncheon Street and its
occupants. There is the Colonel's portrait, mentioned on
twenty different pages. The picture's "stern features" over
and over again recall the man who built this strange house
and whose spirit has always dominated it. There is the map
of "the Pyncheon territory to the eastward," another token
of the family's decline. Linked with the map and the portrait
are the many references to hidden treasure in the house.
These three separate motifs become intertwined and the
hope which they offer collapses with the falling of the picture when Holgrave finds the secret spring—revealing the
worthless deed to the eastern empire. It would be interesting
but scarcely worth the space, to follow these motifs through
the story. Their recurring appearance is part of and helps
to establish the rhythmic sweep of the novel.

As delightful a story as any of Hawthorne's is "Feathertop," and one of the most delightful elements in the story
is Mother Rigby's repeated invocation of the devil, " 'Dickon,
a coal for my pipe.' " Mother Rigby calls for the light four
times (beginning with the first line of the story), and
Feathertop calls for it once. This rhythmic device is so effective that had Hawthorne failed to use it the last time we
should be much disappointed. But Hawthorne repeats it at
the very end of the story: " 'Dickon,' cried she, in her high,
sharp tone, 'another coal for my pipe.' " The story is nicely
rounded off. Another device which is frequently repeated
in this story is the glittering of the star on Feathertop's coat.
When the witch drapes an old plum-colored coat on her

scarecrow's wooden bones: "On the left breast was a round hole, whence either a star of nobility had been rent away, or else the hot heart of some former wearer had scorched it through and through." [IV, 315] This is the first mention of the star, conspicuous for its absence. Once Feathertop emerges in all his glory, the star is seen to glisten on his coat. A little later one of the townspeople asks: " 'Do you see the star at his breast?' " His companion answers: " 'Nay; it is too bright to be seen.' " [IV, 332-33] On the next page, a lady who is looking on cries out: " 'And, bless me, how bright his star is! It positively shoots out flames!' " On page 336, someone adds: " 'Why, as he turns about, the star on his breast is all ablaze.' " Three pages later, Hawthorne says that "the star on Feathertop's breast had scintillated actual flames, and threw a flickering gleam upon the wall, the ceiling, and the floor." After two more pages we read: "the star kept coruscating on Feathertop's breast . . ." and later "His star . . . glowed at that instant with an unutterable splendor." Even after Feathertop sadly returned to his mother, "the star still flamed upon his breast." This star gleams through "Feathertop" as Owen Warland's work-lamp shines through "The Artist of the Beautiful" or as laughter echoes through "Young Goodman Brown." It is set off against the darkness of Mother Rigby's witchcraft and the drabness of the scarecrow's real nature.

There is a rhythmic repetition in "Rappaccini's Daughter" which has an intangible but forceful effect. By breathing poison over a long period of time, Beatrice Rappaccini becomes immune to its effect but she herself acquires a breath which is poisonous. The words *breath* and *breathe* (and their various forms) are consequently important in the story, and they constitute a rhythmic motif. They appear twenty-five times in the fifty pages; but the rhythm is that of Whitman rather than of Longfellow. It is a rhythm which is appropriate to prose. Although a reader may not notice these words as he runs through the story, and although he may

not be conscious of the rhythm, it is there and undoubtedly
has a strong emotional effect. This matter would scarcely be
worth mentioning if it were an isolated example. But there
are many such rhythms in Hawthorne.

Donatello's animal nature is a rhythmic motif in *The
Marble Faun*. We hear of it first at the beginning of the
novel, in reference to the Praxiteles statue: "The animal
nature, indeed, is the most essential part of the Faun's composition." Then, in the next chapter, Donatello is carefully
related to the Faun, and he, too, is described as being "so full
of animal life." When the young Italian first saw the haunting figure of Miriam's model, this quality flared up in him,
and he showed a marked prejudice against the man: "It
resembled not so much a human dislike or hatred, as one
of those instinctive, unreasoning antipathies which the lower
animals sometimes display, and which generally prove more
trustworthy than the acutest insight into character." [IX, 45]
Later, Hawthorne describes Donatello again as "an animal,"
". . . a creature in a state of development less than what
mankind has attained, yet more perfect within itself for that
very deficiency." [IX, 104] In the grounds of the Villa Borghese, Donatello and Miriam are playing together and Hawthorne speaks of "animal spirits, like Donatello's" and when
the boy again sees the model who has been haunting Miriam,
he again becomes enraged: "His lips were drawn apart so as
to disclose his set teeth, thus giving him a look of animal
rage, which we seldom see except in persons of the simplest
and rudest natures." [IX, 122] Kenyon senses this peculiar
characteristic and speaks to Hilda of Donatello's "animal
nature" while they are walking on the Pincian. The next
time Donatello sees the model, he wants to drown him, and
Miriam tries to calm the boy with a tone "such as she might
have used in taming down the wrath of a faithful hound."
[IX, 205] After the model's death, Donatello loses much of
his energetic nature. While they are viewing the monk on
his bier, Kenyon notices that Donatello is different: "the

fine, fresh glow of animal spirits had departed out of his face." [IX, 251] We hear nothing more of this quality in the Count of Monte Beni until the beginning of Book Two, when Kenyon is studying the genealogy of the Monte Beni family. He reflects that the mythical fauns are "capable of a savage fierceness," and learns that among the earlier Monte Benis the "animal spirits" were noticeable. Later, when Kenyon is making a model for the bust of Donatello, he finds that quite unintentionally he has given "the countenance a distorted and violent look, combining animal fierceness with intelligent hatred." [x, 86] The motif ends here. Hawthorne, as he does sometimes but not often, has failed to develop it further.

Several sequences in *The Blithedale Romance* promise to become significant prefigurations, but fail. Two of them, however, constitute rhythmic motifs which have artistic value. Zenobia's ever-present flower gleams with more or less regularity through the novel. We first see the flower when Coverdale meets Zenobia:

> Her hair, which was dark, glossy, and of singular abundance, was put up rather soberly and primly—without curls, or other ornament, except a single flower. It was an exotic of rare beauty, and as fresh as if the hothouse gardner had just clipt it from the stem. That flower has struck deep root into my memory. I can both see it and smell it, at this moment. So brilliant, so rare, so costly as it must have been, and yet enduring only for a day, it was more indicative of the pride and pomp which had a luxuriant growth in Zenobia's character than if a great diamond had sparkled among her hair. [VIII, 16-17]

Hawthorne suggests a bit of symbolism when later, in the same chapter, he refers to this blossom:

> Looking at herself in the glass, and perceiving that her one magnificent flower had grown rather languid (probably by being exposed to the fervency of the kitchen fire), she flung it on the floor, as unconcernedly as a village girl would throw away a faded violet. The action seemed proper

to her character, although, methought, it would still more have befitted the bounteous nature of this beautiful woman to scatter fresh flowers from her hand, and to revive faded ones by her touch. [VIII, 25]

The flower, and a lengthy discussion of it, appears again in chapter six. Coverdale calls it a talisman and says again that it affects his imagination because "this favorite ornament was actually a subtle expression of Zenobia's character." Perhaps for contrast, as well as for characterization, Hawthorne has Zenobia decorate Priscilla with flowers, in chapter eight. Whereas Zenobia's personal flowers are rare and exotic, those she gives Priscilla are quite the opposite: anemones, columbines, violets, everlasting flowers, and cherry blossoms. But, Coverdale adds: "As for herself, she [Zenobia] scorned the rural buds and leaflets, and wore nothing but her invariable flower of the tropics." In chapter ten, old Moodie refers to her as the lady with "the magnificent flower in her hair." There is a reflection of Zenobia's flower when, in chapter fourteen, Coverdale observes that Priscilla "appeared to be tossed aside by her other friends, or carelessly let fall, like a flower which they had done with." After Coverdale leaves Blithedale and goes to the city, chapter eighteen, he sees Zenobia in a window opposite his hotel: "She had, as usual, a flower in her hair, brilliant and of rare variety, else it had not been Zenobia." In the next chapter, when he calls on her, he notes the flower; but this time it is "a flower exquisitely imitated in jeweller's work, and imparting the last touch that transformed Zenobia into a work of art." This is the last direct reference to Zenobia's flower until just before her death. There is an indirect suggestion at the end of chapter twenty-two. After Coverdale hears Moodie's story, he exclaims: " 'Priscilla—poor, pallid flower!—was either snatched from Zenobia's hand, or flung wilfully away!' " This refers to Professor Westervelt's recapture of Priscilla. Shortly before she dies, Zenobia removes the jewelled flower from her hair and hands it to Coverdale. This deed, he says, "struck me as the act of a queen, when worsted in combat, discrowning herself." She requests Coverdale to give the flower to Priscilla for her sake. With this malicious gallantry, the flower motif is completed. Hawthorne might have used the flower in some manner in connection with Zenobia's drowning. From the point of view of its use as a motif, such a change might have been an improvement; but as a symbol, the flower has served its purpose.

Less successful is that of Priscilla's purses. It is disappointing because nothing comes of it. The repeated mention of the purses, although it falls short of being the prefiguration we think it is to be, is still a rhythmic sequence. Four times during the novel there are mentions of the purse: in chapters five, ten, sixteen, and twenty-one. We see the purse when Coverdale observes Priscilla working on it during the first evening at the farm. "I wondered," he says, "if it were not a symbol of Priscilla's own mystery." The next reference to a purse merely serves to relate Moodie to Priscilla. The third is when Priscilla wants to give Coverdale a purse as a keepsake. The last reference shows old Moodie trying to sell one. While this recurring detail may have some of the value of the other motifs in helping to unify the story by rhythmic repetition (and the purse appears with astonishing regularity), it is not by nature a decorative detail, such as the flower was. We therefore expect the repetition to lead to something, and we are disappointed when it does not.

Two other sequences in *The Blithedale Romance* are worth nothing because they are undeveloped. They are interesting examples of details not extended far enough to become real rhythmic motifs. In chapter four and again in chapter seven (only thirty-four pages apart) occur references to Priscilla's clasped hands: "she dropped down upon her knees, clasped her hands, and gazed piteously into Zenobia's face." [viii, 35] and later "she drew it [the letter] back, and held it against her bosom, with both hands clasped over it, in a way that had probably grown habitual to her." [viii, 69] The first mention of the clasped hands would have meant little if the second had not come so soon upon it. But they are close together and the emphasis given to the second seems to make it important. The reader is similarly disappointed by another brief sequence. In chapter eight and chapter nine (twenty-four pages apart) Hawthorne makes tantalizing statements about Priscilla: "But, all at once, midway to Hollingsworth, she paused, looked round about her, towards the river, the road, the woods, and back towards us, appearing to listen, as if she heard someone calling her name, and knew not precisely in what direction." [VIII, 82] When Zenobia's attention is called to this she reports that she has "seen the girl do that identical thing once or twice before." A few pages later, the author notes: "And then came that unintelligible gesture, when she seemed to be listening to a distant voice." [VIII, 106] Although Hawthorne may have intended this to be only an indication of Priscilla's strange and incomprehensible character, he has disappointed the reader because a potentially effective motif has been left hanging. It seems probable to me that he originally intended this gesture to be related in some way to the suggestion of mesmerism which appears from time to time in the novel. Either he forgot to develop it or intentionally dropped it.

Rhythm, as I said at the beginning of this chapter, can be used for its own sake or it can be used to point-up and emphasize some detail. Hawthorne frequently uses it for this latter purpose. I have called this kind of rhythmic sequence *prefiguration*,[1] largely to avoid the term *foreshadowing* which is used so often in dramatic criticism. He focuses the reader's attention by this means just as a dramatist drops hints, along the way, of a forthcoming action; or, for that

---

[1] Hawthorne himself uses the word, as a verb, in *The Scarlet Letter*. He is speaking of Hester's jailor who "prefigured and represented in his aspect the whole dismal severity of the Puritanic code of law, which it was his business to administer in its final and closest application to the offender." [VI, 92] We can see from this that Hawthorne uses the term much as I do, as a reflection in advance, if such a thing can be imagined.

matter, just as a stage-director guides his audience's attention by the way in which he points-up a subsequent action by emphasizing an earlier version of the same or a similar action. A painter often emphasizes some detail in his picture by repeating that detail, or certain aspects of it, in other parts of the composition. He can control our attention by sequence in color or line movement: thus he is prefiguring either the color or the line of the detail which he wants to emphasize. Prefiguration, then, is a sequence which is not only rhythmic but which at the same time points toward something. I think Hawthorne uses this device quite consciously.[2]

In "Young Goodman Brown" we find a prefiguration which, though it is not of the simplest variety, is neat and clearly seen. Faith, Goodman Brown's wife, is pictured in the first paragraph of the story as wearing pink ribbons in her cap. A few lines down the page we read again of "Faith with the pink ribbons," and farther down on the same page we read of the young man looking back and seeing "the head of Faith still peeping after him, with a melancholy air, in spite of her pink ribbons." There are two more references to Faith during the next half-dozen pages; and though the ribbons are not mentioned, the reader is certain to think of them. Then, at the turning-point of the story, we read:

> There was a scream, drowned immediately in a louder murmur of voices, fading into far-off laughter, as the dark cloud swept away, leaving the clear and silent sky above Goodman Brown. But something fluttered lightly down through the air and caught on the branch of a tree. The young man seized it, and beheld a pink ribbon. [IV, 114-115]

We would not have thought much of this ribbon if Hawthorne had not mentioned it so often at the beginning of the

---

[2] In his note-books, Hawthorne comments on the theme of a Blue Beard tale which William Storey talked to him about: "Were I to take up the story, I would create an interest by suggesting a secret in the first chamber, which would develop itself more and more in every successive hall of the great palace, and lead the wife irresistibly to the chamber of horrors." [XXI, 285] I believe that Hawthorne is thinking about what we are calling *prefiguration*.

story. But the prefiguration does not stop here. When Goodman Brown sees the ribbons falling from the air, he turns himself over to the devil. At this point, the pink of the ribbons acquires a more sinister shade. In his mad rush through the forest the young man sees "a red light before him," which is the burning trees. When he and Faith are admitted into the unholy gathering to be baptized, Hawthorne writes: "A basin was hollowed, naturally, in the rock. Did it contain water, reddened by the lurid light? or was it blood? or, perchance, a liquid flame?" [IV, 122] The pink of the ribbons and the red of the light both prefigure the red liquid in the baptismal font. It is at this point that Goodman Brown calls out, " 'Faith! Faith!' " and the dream, or whatever it was, ends. We see here a double focusing. The falling of the ribbon, which marks Goodman's loss of faith, is pointed-up by the previous mentions of the ribbon; and this whole motif merges into another prefiguration pointing-up the basin of liquid fire. The reader may not be conscious of this device while he is reading the story, but neither is the observer of a picture necessarily conscious of the composition which leads his eye inevitably to a point at which the artist wants his attention focused.

"Roger Malvin's Burial" is not one of Hawthorne's best stories, but from our point of view it is saved from obscurity by prefiguration as artistic as any in the author's work. In the second paragraph:

> The early sunbeams hovered cheerfully upon the tree-tops, beneath which two weary and wounded men had stretched their limbs the night before. . . . On a tract of several acres around this rock, oaks and other hard-wood trees had supplied the place of the pines which were the usual growth of the land; and a young and vigorous sapling stood close beside the travellers. [V, 133]

(Only two sentences have been omitted.) The force of these lines is not immediately apparent. But in the next sentence, beginning the third paragraph, Hawthorne repeats and thereby turns a simple image into a significant motif:

The severe wound of the elder man had probably de-
prived him of sleep; for, so soon as the first ray of sunshine
rested on the top of the highest tree, he reared himself pain-
fully from his recumbent posture and sat erect. [v, 133]

The high-light on the treetop is now clear and distinct. The
repetition not only serves as a literary transition, but also
establishes a prefiguration. The last sentence of the first
quotation links "the young and vigorous sapling" with the
sunlight on the highest tree, relating the sapling to the prefiguration. These two are not necessarily the same tree, but
they are related, artistically. As the story progresses, Reuben
prepares for his departure:

Then climbing to the summit of the rock, which on one side
was rough and broken, he bent the oak-sapling downward,
and bound his handkerchief to the topmost branch. [v, 141]

Hawthorne has further strengthened the link between the
sapling and the sunlit treetop. We are justified, now, in expecting these images, which have been combined into a single
motif, to be used again. After a dozen pages (during which
Reuben has grown to manhood and acquired a family) Hawthorne once more brings in the tree:

The sapling to which he had bound the blood-stained symbol
of his vow had increased and strengthened into an oak, far
indeed from its maturity, but with no mean spread of
shadowy branches. There was one singularity observable in
this tree which made Reuben tremble. The middle and lower
branches were in luxuriant life, and an excess of vegetation
had fringed the trunk almost to the ground; but a blight
had apparently stricken the upper part of the oak, and the
very topmost bough was withered, sapless, and utterly dead.
Reuben remembered how the little banner had fluttered on
that topmost bough, when it was green and lovely, eighteen
years before. Whose guilt had blasted it? [v, 160-61]

The prefiguration and symbolism are not yet completed, because Hawthorne's sense of the value of symbolism demands
that he make more of this tree. His artistic consciousness in-
forms him that he cannot use the symbol again without

another prefiguration to keep the whole aesthetically intact. This he gives us a few lines down the page, when Dorcas, Reuben's wife, is making camp:

> It had a strange aspect, that one little spot of homely comfort, in the desolate heart of Nature. The sunshine yet lingered upon the higher branches of the trees that grew on rising ground; but the shadows of evening had deepened into the hollow where the encampment was made ... [v, 161]

The "strange aspect" and the "shadows of evening" link the symbol with the motif. From now on we can expect the worst from the grown-up sapling. On the last page of the story, the action, which repetition has now made inevitable, occurs:

> At that moment the withered topmost bough of the oak loosened itself in the stilly air, and fell in soft, light fragments upon the rock, upon the leaves, upon Reuben, upon his wife and child, and upon Roger Malvin's bones. [v, 165]

Again Hawthorne has held a story together by the rhythm of prefiguration. Sheer artistry has told us what to expect and has met our expectations.

Prefiguration is used in *The House of the Seven Gables* to introduce Clifford. A motif, the Malbone miniature, aided by other comments, heralds Clifford's arrival. We see the miniature almost as soon as we see Hepzibah. One of her first actions is to unlock a secret drawer in her writing-desk and take out the little picture:

> It is a likeness of a young man, in a silken dressing-gown of an old fashion, the soft richness of which is well adapted to the countenance of reverie, with its full, tender lips, and beautiful eyes, that seem to indicate not so much capacity of thought, as gentle and voluptuous emotion. Of the possessor of such features we shall have a right to ask nothing, except that he would take the rude world easily, and make himself happy in it. [vii, 41-42]

At the sight of the Colonel's portrait, in chapter four, Hepzibah thinks again of her precious miniature; and Hawthorne again describes the lips and eyes as they are pictured by

Malbone. We must interrupt the sequence here to point out two remarks which, though they do not refer to the minia-ture, are part of the total prefiguration. The first is a whispered question by Uncle Venner: " 'When do you ex-pect him home?' " The second comes a few pages later and is Hepzibah's comment when Phoebe arrives: " 'If Clifford were to find her here, it might disturb him!' " The miniature again appears, a few pages later in chapter five, when Hepzi-bah shows it to Phoebe, who examines it carefully. Then, when Clifford makes his appearance at Hepzibah's elaborate breakfast-party, Phoebe recognizes him: "She saw that the person before her must have been the original of the beautiful miniature in her cousin Hepzibah's possession." [VII, 151] With this, the introduction is complete. As we come to know Clifford throughout the novel, we agree that the miniature has justly presented him.

It is worth noting that Hawthorne uses the same device to acquaint Phoebe with Judge Jaffray Pyncheon. Holgrave, the daguerreotypist, has shown her a sample of his craft and Phoebe immediately recognizes a likeness between the face in this miniature and the one in the Colonel's portrait. Hol-grave assures her that "this is a modern face, and one which you will very probably meet." When she does meet the Judge, she recognizes him as she has Clifford:

> Then, all at once, it struck Phoebe that this very Judge Pyncheon was the original of the miniature which the daguerreotypist had shown her in the garden, and that the hard, stern, relentless look, now on his face, was the same that the sun had so inflexibly persisted in bringing out. [VII, 171]

We are not dealing, in this study, with the subject-matter of Hawthorne's works, with problems of morality or with the meaning of the stories, but it will be profitable occasionally to note the ways in which he brings out the point of a story. Prefiguration is used for this purpose in "The Birthmark." The meaning of the tale is summed-up in the last paragraph:

Thus ever does the gross fatality of earth exult in its invariable triumph over the immortal essence which, in this dim sphere of half development, demands the completeness of a higher state. Yet, had Aylmer reached a profounder wisdom, he need not thus have flung away the happiness which would have woven his mortal life of the selfsame texture with the celestial. The momentary circumstance was too strong for him; he failed to look beyond the shadowy scope of time, and, living once for all in eternity, to find the perfect future in the present. [IV, 76-77]

Georgianna has had to die because Aylmer's attempt to remove the birthmark, though it was successful, has killed her. He has tried to improve on nature. Hawthorne focuses our attention and our interest on this failure by means of prefiguration. The first element in the series appears shortly after the opening of the story:

"I feel myself fully competent to render this dear cheek as faultless as its fellow; and then, most beloved, what will be my triumph when I shall have corrected what Nature left imperfect in her fairest work!" [IV, 55-56]

And Georgianna replies, " 'And, Aylmer, spare me not, though you should find the birth-mark take refuge in my heart at last.' " This is the first suggestion of his desire to better nature and of his possible failure. A page later, Hawthorne calls nature "our great creative mother." "She permits us, indeed, to mar, but seldom to mend. . . ." Farther on in the story, when Aylmer is trying to soothe Georgianna, "to release her mind from the burden of actual things," he performs some scientific wonders for her. He makes a flower sprout and grow before her eyes. Aylmer's comment, when the flower suddenly dies, is that the stimulus was too powerful. (This, of course, is a direct prefiguration of Georgianna's death.) The scientist shows his wife a strong drug, a few drops of which would wash away freckles and a "stronger infusion would take the blood out of the cheek, and leave the rosiest beauty a pale ghost." [IV, 64] When his wife asks if this is to be used to remove her birthmark, he replies, "This is merely superficial. Your case demands a remedy that shall go deeper." Normally, one would think, a solution which "would leave the rosiest beauty a pale ghost" would be dangerous, and anything which went deeper would kill. But Aylmer has not yet reached the state which the author later calls "a profounder wisdom." While Georgianna is thumbing through her husband's note-books she begins to realize more acutely his scientific skill as well as his ruthlessness and ambition. "Much as he had accomplished, she could not but observe that his most splendid successes were almost invariably failures, if compared with the ideal at which he aimed." [IV, 66] She hopes, though with some doubt, that his experiment on her will be successful, not so much for herself as for him:

> . . . and, with her whole spirit she prayed that, for a single moment, she might satisfy his highest and deepest conception. Longer than one moment she well knew it could not be; for his spirit was ever on the march, ever ascending, and each instant required something that was beyond the scope of the instant before. [IV, 71-72]

This is another direct prefiguration of Aylmer's temporary success and Georgianna's subsequent death. As Aylmer hands her the goblet of medicine designed to remove her birthmark, he says that it is perfect. " 'Unless all my science have deceived me, it cannot fail.' " As Georgianna drinks, Aylmer states: " 'There is no taint of imperfection on thy spirit. Thy sensible frame, too, shall soon be all perfect.' " This time, as in his other experiments, "he failed to look beyond the shadowy scope of Time." The experiment works perfectly. It is the old story: the operation was a beautiful success, but the patient died.

The prefiguration of the Veiled Lady in *The Blithedale Romance* is a particularly good one. There are four references to her in the first chapter of the novel. Coverdale has just returned from seeing this "phenomenon in the mesmeric line" when old Moodie, while on the subject of Priscilla and

Blithedale, asks him about Zenobia. The answer which Hawthorne puts into Coverdale's mouth is revealing:

> "Zenobia, by the bye, as I suppose you know, is merely her public name; a sort of mask in which she comes before the world, retaining all the privileges of privacy,—a contrivance, in short, like the white drapery of the Veiled Lady, only a little more transparent." [viii, 5]

Zenobia and Priscilla are thus linked to Moodie and the Veiled Lady in the first chapter, although the reader at this point does not realize this relationship. We hear nothing more of this mysterious entertainer until chapter six when Coverdale, unconscious of his omniscience, says, " 'Zenobia is an enchantress! . . . She is the sister of the Veiled Lady.' " In chapter thirteen, "Zenobia's Legend," a story of the Veiled Lady, Zenobia makes a number of allusions which suggest that Priscilla and this astonishing figure are one and the same person; but her remarks are vague and not completely understood. She also suggests a connection between Professor Westervelt and the Veiled Lady. Hawthorne very ingeniously weaves all these relationships together in this strange story. In chapter twenty-two, Moodie, without using the phrase *Veiled Lady,* suggests her in his story of Fauntleroy, when he speaks of Westervelt's interest in Priscilla:

> They [the people of the neighborhood] averred that the strange gentleman was a wizard, and that he had taken advantage of Priscilla's lack of earthly substance to subject her to himself, as his familiar spirit, through whose medium he gained cognizance of whatever happened, in regions near or remote. The boundaries of his power were defined by the verge of the pit of Tartarus on the one hand, and the third sphere of the celestial world on the other. . . . But, after every possible deduction, there remained certain very mysterious points about the stranger's character, as well as the connection that he established with Priscilla. Its nature at that period was even less understood than now, when miracles of this kind have grown so absolutely stale, that I would gladly, if the truth allowed, dismiss the whole matter from my narrative. [viii, 268-69]

However indirect this reference may be, it is a strong beat in the rhythmic sequence of the Veiled Lady. There is nothing, however, indirect about the next chapter, twenty-three. It is the culmination of the motif, the image toward which the preceding references have pointed. At last the Veiled Lady is unveiled and shown to be Priscilla.

Several small prefigurations are scattered through *The Marble Faun,* but they are not extensive, possibly one reason for the novel's lack of artistic unity. The most effective of these short sequences is the series of suggestions leading up to the killing of Miriam's model. In Book One, chapter eighteen is entitled "On the Edge of a Precipice." In this chapter the four principal characters are viewing the Forum by night. They have come to the spot where, according to the vague legends, Metius Curtius sacrificed his life to save Rome by leaping into a gulf. Kenyon philosophizes on this subject at some length, stressing the elements of death and destruction. Hawthorne continues the discussion by talking about the impenetrable chasm between the spirit of ancient and of modern Rome. The group later moves on to a spot, on one side of which "rose the great height of the palace," and on the other sides "nothing but the parapet, which as it now appeared was built right on the edge of a steep precipice." Kenyon tells the group that from this place, one of the sides of the Tarpeian rock, "many a Roman caught his last glimpse of his native city." This is the famous Traitor's Leap, and Miriam is deeply moved by its history and significance:

> "It would be a fatal fall, still," she said to herself, looking over the parapet, and shuddering as her eye measured the depth. "Yes; surely yes! Even without the weight of an overburdened heart, a human body would fall heavily enough upon those stones to shake all its joints asunder. How soon it would be over!" [ix, 235]

Those who have leaped over the precipice in the past, she says, were men who "cumbered the world. . . . Men whose lives were the bane of their fellow-creatures." When we read that a figure suddenly appears out of the darkness and that Miriam recognizes him as her "strange persecutor," we know what is going to happen. It happens; and the model joins all those others whose "lives were the bane of their fellow-creatures."

Miriam's arrival at Monte Beni is prefigured, though not too cleverly. The motif begins at the end of the next-to-the-last chapter in Book One. Kenyon is distressed at Donatello's melancholy and exclaims to himself: " 'How a woman's face would brighten it up!' " On the last page of the first book, Hawthorne notes that some unknown person has rewarded the beggars who had been stationed outside the castle. He does not tell who it is; it might be Miriam. In chapter one of Book Two, Kenyon again expresses the feeling that a woman might cheer Donatello and his old house. In chapter two, when Kenyon once more comments on the need of a woman at Monte Beni, old Tomaso says, " 'Ah; we will wait a little longer.' " A few pages later, in chapter four of Book Two, "a woman's voice was heard, singing in a low, sad strain." Whether or not either Kenyon or Donatello recognizes it, we are not told, although certainly both suspect. At the end of the following chapter, Tomaso tells Kenyon, " 'The signorina would speak with you.' " Not until chapter six does Miriam actually make her appearance, even though we are led to believe that she has been in the castle for several days. Other prefigurations in *The Marble Faun* are worth listing, though they are not well enough developed to justify our tracing them: Miriam's losing her way in the catacombs is sketchily prefigured; the extinction of Hilda's lamp is negatively pointed-up by frequent references to the need for keeping it burning; and the rosebud which Hilda tosses to Kenyon in the Corso is an echo of a previous similar action.

A prefiguration in "Ethan Brand" is effective, if not very subtle. Subtlety in prefiguration, indeed, is not always a virtue; a prefiguration may be obvious and still be good. However, I think we prefer that a prefiguration be somewhat

delicate and at least interwoven in the fabric of the story so
that it does not glare too boldly. It must be remembered, too,
that the more we think about prefigurations and the more
we look for them the more obvious they seem. This one in
"Ethan Brand" is more open than some others, but it cannot be called obtrusive. A vague hint as to the outcome is
given when the author is reflecting on Ethan at the beginning
of the story. He tells us that the lime-kiln has remained un-
changed since that time, years back, when Ethan "had
thrown his dark thoughts into the intense glow of its furnace, and melted them, as it were, into one thought that took
possession of his life." [III, 113] When Ethan comes back to
the foot of Graylock, "he fixed his eyes . . . intently upon the
brightness of the furnace, as if he beheld, or expected to behold, some object worthy of note within it." [III, 116] Just
before the end of the first part of the tale, Bartram is described as watching Ethan and half expecting him "to plunge
bodily into the flames, and thus vanish from the sight of
man." [III, 122] The prefiguration is not used again until
near the end of the middle section. Ethan, annoyed by the
taunts of the show-box man, sternly says to him, " 'Peace . . .
or get thee into the furnace yonder!' " [III, 131] When Ethan
urges the lime-burner and his son to go to bed and leave him
alone to watch the kiln, we suspect the outcome—but this
cannot be counted as a prefiguration. The next and last recurrence of the motif is just before the deed is accomplished:

> Ethan Brand stood erect, and raised his arms on high.
> The blue flames played upon his face, and imparted the wild
> and ghastly light which alone could have suited its expres-
> sion; it was that of a fiend on the verge of plunging into his
> gulf of intensest torment. [III, 136-37]

This story then offers an unusual device, a kind of "post-
figuration." In the morning, Bartram, fearing that Ethan
has let the fire go out, growls, " 'If I catch the fellow here-
abouts again, I shall feel like tossing him into the furnace!' "
[III, 139] A horrible but artistic echo!

A different kind of prefiguration is found in "Feathertop."
The climax of the story occurs when Feathertop sees himself
reflected in the mirror:

> By and by Feathertop paused, and throwing himself into
> an imposing attitude, seemed to summon the fair girl to
> survey his figure and resist him longer if she could. . . .
> The maiden raised her eyes and suffered them to linger
> upon her companion with a bashful and admiring gaze.
> Then, as if desirous of judging what value her own simple
> comeliness might have side by side with so much brilliancy,
> she cast a glance towards the full-length looking-glass in
> front of which they happened to be standing. It was one of
> the truest plates in the world and incapable of flattery. No
> sooner did the images therein reflected meet Polly's eye
> than she shrieked, shrank from the stranger's side, gazed at
> him for a moment in the wildest dismay, and sank insensible
> upon the floor. Feathertop likewise had looked towards the
> mirror, and there beheld, not the glittering mockery of his
> outside show, but a picture of the sordid patchwork of his
> real composition, stripped of all witchcraft. [IV, 341-42]

Let us look back half a dozen pages and see how Hawthorne
prefigures this calamity. Polly is preparing to meet her
father's distinguished visitor:

> This young lady had caught a glimpse of the glistening
> stranger while standing at the threshold, and had forthwith
> put on a laced cap, a string of beads, her finest kerchief,
> and her stiffest damask petticoat in preparation for the inter-
> view. Hurrying from her chamber to the parlor, she had ever
> since been viewing herself in the large looking-glass and
> practising pretty airs—now a smile, now a ceremonious
> dignity of aspect, and now a softer smile than the former,
> kissing her hand likewise, tossing her head, and managing
> her fan; while within the mirror an unsubstantial little maid
> repeated every gesture and did all the foolish things that
> Polly did, but without making her ashamed of them. In
> short, it was the fault of pretty Polly's ability rather than
> her will if she failed to be as complete an artifice as the
> illustrious Feathertop himself; and, when she thus tampered
> with her own simplicity, the witch's phantom might well
> hope to win her. [IV, 336-37]

The reader who insists on looking only at context, at subject-matter, may, if he wishes, point out the moral symbolism in these passages. But for us who are interested in form, it is as good an example of prefiguration as we shall find in Hawthorne.

Hawthorne's stories are not equally artistic. In "The Man of Adamant," for example, prefiguration is weak. It is transparent, like the composition of a picture which is too obviously composed. The title itself deprives the outcome of some of its effect. When Hawthorne exposes everything on the third page of his story, he spoils it. He tells us that from the roof of Richard Digby's cave dripped a substance which turned into adamant whatever it fell upon. Then Richard is said to have some kind of disease which is slowly changing "his fleshy heart into stone." This is too much. Any suspense the story might have had is ruined. Another prefiguration in this story, however, is successful. Near the beginning, Hawthorne describes the cave:

> If nature meant this remote and dismal cavern for the use of man, it could only be to bury in its gloom the victims of a pestilence, and then to block up its mouth with stones, and avoid the spot forever after. [iii, 228]

At the end of the tale, the farmer, whose children discovered the cave, begins "to heap stones into the mouth of the cavern." It is completely sealed and bushes grow over its former entrance. "Yet grown people avoid the spot, nor do children play there." [iii, 238] This is a good prefiguration. It differs from the other in this story in that it points ahead without revealing too much. Prefiguration, if carefully handled, can contribute to suspense; it need not destroy it.

"The Devil in Manuscript" offers a neat and humorous little variation of the device of prefiguration. Oberon, a writer, has determined to burn his manuscripts. The narrator thinks this is a good idea because "the tales would make a more brilliant appearance in the fire than anywhere else." When he sees the papers burning, Oberon is relieved and delighted. Under the influence of his relief and of four "brimming bumpers" of champagne, he screams out his delight:

"Ring out the bells! A city is on fire. See!—destruction roars through my dark forests, while the lakes boil up in steaming billows, and the mountains are volcanoes, and the sky kindles with a lurid brightness! All elements are but one pervading flame!" [III, 248]

Shortly after this outburst, the two friends hear the fire alarm: there is a real fire somewhere in the city. Hawthorne, the narrator, has forebodings and suspicions. Then Oberon, too, realizes what has happened:

"My tales!" cried Oberon. "The chimney! The roof! The Fiend has gone forth by night, and startled thousands in fear and wonder from their beds! Here I stand,—a triumphant author! Huzza! Huzza! My brain has set the town on fire! Huzza!" [III, 251]

An amusing use of prefiguration!

5. Color, Light-&-Shade, Sound

"All art, therefore, appeals primarily to the senses, and the artistic aim when expressing itself in written words must also make its appeal through the senses, if its high desire is to reach the secret springs of responsive emotions. It must strenuously aspire to the plasticity of sculpture, to the color of painting, and to the magic suggestiveness of music. . ."—JOSEPH CONRAD, Preface to *The Nigger of the Narcissus.*

E VEN A CURSORY reading of Hawthorne will convince the reader that he has a *graphic* mind. He thinks in pictures. The note-books are packed with descriptive passages suggestive of keen observation, and the stories and novels depend for much of their effectiveness on pictures of things and people and places. Joseph Conrad tells us that his own job as a writer is to make us see things: "My task which I am trying to achieve is by the power of the written word to make you hear, to make you feel—it is, before all, to make you see."[1] These words might almost have been Hawthorne's. A writer, particularly a romantic writer, relies heavily on the appeal to the senses through the creation of images. Color, light-and-shade, and sound are his principal means. Description is the method.

Hawthorne tells us in his note-books that "pictorial art is capable of something more like magic . . . than poetry, or any other mode of developing the beautiful." [XXII, 77] He is greatly interested in the art of painting, as we can see from the note-books and from the frequent references to painting

---

[1] The Preface to *The Nigger of the Narcissus* (Garden City, Doubleday, Doran and Co., 1931), p. xiii.

in *The Blithedale Romance, The House of the Seven Gables, The Marble Faun,* and several of the short stories. In a letter to his wife, he wrote:

> I never owned a picture in my life; yet pictures have been among the earthly possessions (and they are spiritual possessions, too) which I most coveted. . . . I have often felt that I could be a painter; only I am sure I could never handle a brush . . .[2]

He was evidently born with some enthusiasm for painting, and gradually developed a little taste and critical judgment. (Perhaps Sophia Peabody Hawthorne's influence helps to account for this development, although her interests did not seem to have a marked effect on Hawthorne's aesthetic growth.) The most extensive discussion of painters and painting is in the English section of the note-books. He visited the Manchester exhibition many times, and after one visit, made interesting observations (1857). All English painters, he feels, are like Hogarth in that they are best at portraying low life. "They cannot paint anything high, heroic, and ideal." Lawrence has a "sort of grace, which you feel to be a trick, and therefore get disgusted with it." The Pre-Raphaelites who "almost paint even separate hairs" are nearly as good as Hogarth, and Copley and Danby, too, are to be recommended for their realism. At first Hawthorne did not care for Turner, although later he admitted a greater appreciation for him. Vandyke, who "seems to have brought portrait-painting into fashion," is not among his favorites, although he did about as well as anyone could do. He writes of several portraits of Mary of Scotland, "none of which have a gleam of beauty; but the stiff old brushes of these painters could not catch the beautiful." In fact, he is not sure that painted portraits ever give "a genuine idea of the person purporting to be represented." [xxi, 25-37] In portraiture, as in all art, Hawthorne

---

[2] Cited in Julian Hawthorne, *Nathaniel Hawthorne and his Wife* (Boston, James R. Osgood and Co., 1885), I, 211.

seeks accurate and faithful imitation of nature; although in "The Prophetic Pictures" he seems to admire the painter who " 'paints not merely a man's features, but his mind and heart.' "

In spite of his interest and the hours spent looking at pictures, he apparently had little or no technical knowledge of painting. He watched several artists work (chiefly Mr. Thompson) while he was sitting for them, but even that does not seem to have helped. He learned remarkably little about texture, pigments, brush-strokes, design, composition, and other technical factors. His interest in painting seems to have been intuitive, at least entirely natural. He loved colors, and he liked pictures just for the sake of pictures. As I have said before, Hawthorne *thinks* in terms of pictures. Speaking through Oberon, in "The Devil in Manuscript," he says of a story: "My picture, painted in what seemed the loveliest hues, presents nothing but a faded and indistinguishable surface." [III, 246] A story, to him, is a picture. Oberon might well be speaking of Hawthorne's "The Lily's Quest," which is as much like a painting as any story can be. It is a pastoral scene suggesting Claude Lorraine, or Lancret, or Fragonard. It is a "Shepherds of Arcadia" as any one of these men might have painted it. There is the ever-present rambling brook, the rolling landscape, the fluffy foliage, the over-all tone of gray and yellow and green. And there is, to complete the picture, a small neo-classic temple,

> . . . on the summit of the knoll, amid the solemn shadows of the trees, yet often gladdened with bright sunshine. It was built of white marble, with slender and graceful pillars supporting a vaulted dome; and beneath the centre of this dome, upon a pedestal, was a slab of dark-veined marble, on which books and music might be strewn. [II, 296-97]

Nothing is missing. It is an almost perfect transference, in line, form, and color, from the art of painting to the art of prose.

Hawthorne frequently laments that so many fine pictures of the Old Masters have lost their original colors through fading or too much cleaning and varnishing. In Rome, he saw the work of an inconsequential Boston painter, Mr. Wilde, and waxed enthusiastic over the colors: "miracles of color, being as bright as if the light were transmitted through rubies and sapphires." [xxi, 342] He said of Thompson, "I should like his pictures for the mere color, even if they represented nothing." [xxi, 204-205] From Hawthorne, who demanded representation in art, this is loud praise! He liked all colors, particularly red,[3] and he filled his stories with glowing hues, even though sombre tones seem to prevail. Red is undoubtedly the most frequently mentioned color. A comment from the note-books shows his delicate feeling for colors and the differences between them. He has been looking at the windows of York Cathedral, and decides that the modern glass is "far more magnificent, as to brightness of color and material beauty, than the ancient." However, there is something "vulgar, glaring, and impertinent" about the modern glass. "Indeed, in the very coloring, I felt the same difference as between heart's blood and a scarlet dye." [xx, 151]

We have already seen that Hawthorne makes good use of light-and-shade. Like color, light-and-shade, for its plastic value as well as for contrast, is an important and frequently

---

[3] His fondness for red is apparent throughout the stories. A comment from the note-books interestingly reveals his feeling toward that color: "The red light which the sunsets at this season diffuse; there being showery afternoons, but the sun setting bright amid clouds, and diffusing its radiance over those that are scattered in masses all over the sky. It gives a rich tinge to all objects, even to those of sombre hues, yet without changing the hues. The complexions of people are exceedingly enriched by it; they look warm, and kindled with a mild fire. The whole scenery and personages acquire, methinks, a passionate character. A love-scene should be laid on such an evening. The trees and grass have now the brightest possible green, there having been so many showers alternating with such powerful sunshine. There are roses and tulips and honeysuckles, with their sweet perfume; in short, the splendor of a more gorgeous climate than ours might be brought into the picture." (1838) [xviii, 128] This appears to be a note for a story which would evidently have a strong red tinge.

employed artistic device in his writings. He knows how to use it to best advantage. In the Preface to *The House of the Seven Gables* he states that the writer can, if he sees fit, "so manage his atmospherical medium as to bring out or mellow the lights and deepen and enrich the shadows of the picture." [vii, xxi] Miriam, in *The Marble Faun,* explains that artists can control sunlight and use it for whatever effect they wish. [ix, 51] In the note-books, Hawthorne epigrammatically says: "Moonlight is sculpture; sunlight is painting," [xvii, 249]—a statement which does not mean a great deal, but suggests a feeling for the difference between lights. As we go on in this study, we shall see that there is a real artistic sensitivity in his use of both light-and-shade and color.

When we talk about Hawthorne's use of color, we are not speaking merely of description. He uses color for descriptive purposes; but it is a means and not an end. We are not concerned with the accuracy of descriptive phrases such as "a lock of hair, once sable, now discolored with a greenish mould." We do not, at least in this investigation, care about the accuracy or truth of the terms "sable" or "greenish," but rather about the way he uses this particular sable or green. Color is more to Hawthorne than mere pigment for the painting of a description. It is a part of a larger device designed, as Joseph Conrad says, to "reach the secret springs of responsive emotion." It is an emotional element rather than merely a descriptive one. When we were looking at the structure of "Howe's Masquerade," we could not fail to observe its color pattern. The first group of figures is painted without any color except for a touch of red, "the stain of blood," and with no shading. The painting of the second group is colorless, too, but it is varied by spots of white and the glitter of metal. In the third group, we see first the scarlet uniform, then the "rubicund" nose, and then the purple of a velvet suit. The solitary figure at the end of the procession is dark again, with only the gilt of his scabbard for relief. Hawthorne weaves color very carefully in this story: from the blood-red, used as a kind of prophecy, to scarlet, to the tinge of "rubicund," to purple—the shade becomes darker as it progresses—and finally to black, with the touch of gilt for emphasis. He uses color here, as he does in most of his stories, for its emotional and mood value rather than for its intellectual and descriptive value.

Perhaps the most colorful of Hawthorne's stories is "Rappaccini's Daughter." Color-adjectives in this story, it is true, are few: the word *purple* is used six times, *crimson* once, *orange* once, *silver* twice, and there are a half-dozen references to gold and gilt. Although there are comparatively few color-adjectives, "Rappaccini's Daughter" manages to stimulate one of the most colorful images in literature. Color-adjectives are not the only means of suggesting color, as we shall see. When Giovanni Guasconti first looks down on Rappaccini's garden, the author describes it in glowing terms, concluding as follows:

> All about the pool into which the water subsided grew various plants, that seemed to require a plentiful supply of moisture for the nourishment of gigantic leaves, and, in some instances, flowers gorgeously magnificent. There was one shrub in particular, set in a marble vase in the midst of the pool, that bore a profusion of purple blossoms, each of which had the lustre and richness of a gem; and the whole together made a show so resplendent that it seemed enough to illuminate the garden, even had there been no sunshine. [IV, 130]

Hawthorne has located the important plant, indicated its color, and has compared it to a gem. He repeats this picture a few lines later when he tells us that Rappaccini "came to the magnificent plant that hung its purple gems beside the marble fountain." The author echoes this in the voice of Beatrice, "a voice as rich as a tropical sunset, and which made Giovanni, though he knew not why, think of deep hues of purple or crimson, and of perfumes heavily delectable." The purple has now been linked with crimson and likened to a sunset, which is colorful enough. But it is a tropical sunset, and this gives the colors a bizarre and luscious cast—if for no other reason than that most of us have never seen a tropical sunset and therefore imaginatively attribute to it gorgeous and fantastic hues. The same force is at work when Hawthorne later speaks of "the Oriental sunshine of her beauty," the "garden of Persian roses," and "odors richer than those of Araby." This use of connotation is a simple device which most good writers employ. In Hawthorne, however, it is not direct but indirect. He interweaves these suggestive terms with other motifs and thus builds up in our minds a vivid image.

Beatrice's appearance adds further glory to the mass of color:

> Soon there emerged from under a sculptured portal the figure of a young girl, arrayed with as much richness of taste as the most splendid of the flowers, beautiful as the day, and with a bloom so deep and vivid that one shade more would have been too much. [IV, 133]

The "bloom so deep and vivid" tends to repeat the purple of the flowers. In the next definite description of the garden, Hawthorne further builds up the picture:

> The strange plants were basking in the sunshine, and now and then nodding gently to one another, as if in acknowledgement of sympathy and kindred. In the midst, by the shattered fountain, grew the magnificent shrub, with its purple gems clustering all over it; they glowed in the air, and gleamed back again out of the depths of the pool, which thus seemed to overflow with colored radiance from the rich reflection that was steeped in it. [IV, 140]

Now the whole garden, and the purple flower in particular, is so closely related to the gems that further references to gems or jewels will arouse in the reader's mind the total coloring of the garden. Hawthorne takes full advantage of the relationship thus established. A page later he writes of "an analogy between the beautiful girl and the gorgeous shrub that hung its gemlike flowers over the fountain." And shortly after this: "There it blushed, and almost glimmered with the dazzling effect of a precious stone." There are two more uses of the word *purple,* but they are scarcely necessary and serve merely to strengthen the image: Giovanni speaks of " 'the precious purple flower,' " and farther on in the story he observes "a purple print, like that of four small fingers, and the likeness of a slender thumb upon his wrist." The gem motif acquires more and more color as it is repeated. There are "fantasies of a gemlike brilliancy, as if diamonds and rubies sparkled upward among the bubbles of the fountain." [IV, 156] Giovanni speaks of the " 'living gems for the bouquet' "; and by acquiring life, the gems acquire more and more different colors. There are references to "the gemlike flowers," to a "Bouquet that was still gemmed with the morning dewdrops," to the "shrub that bore the gemlike blossoms," and finally Rappaccini's reference to " 'those precious gems to thy sister-shrub.' " The motif lends color to the scene by the variety of its uses.

Not alone by direct color imagery does Hawthorne give color to "Rappaccini's Daughter." Scintillating movement, as we noticed earlier, contributes to this effect. There is a constant play of sunlight and shade. In his painting technique, Hawthorne is an impressionist. He realizes the value of light, and to some extent he paints by means of picturing the reflection of light from objects, as the impressionist painters did. He uses a kind of *pointillisme.* By mixing different spots of color with spots of light and dark he produces the effect of living color which Monet and Sisley so avidly sought.

The Blithedale Romance has its share of color, though perhaps less than one might expect of a pastoral scene. The first spot of color is rather appropriately the "red-tipt nose" of old Moodie. In chapter eight, "A Modern Arcadia," there is violet and scarlet in the flowers with which Zenobia decks Priscilla, two references to blue clothes, and a reference to the earth being "a green garden, blossoming with many colored delights." Moodie's scarlet tip is again mentioned. The woods around the farm are likened to a "green cathedral." The grapes in Coverdale's hermitage glow with the crimson of blood. Zenobia uses scarlet shawls in her amateur theatricals. Crimson curtains and the "red glow of the kitchen-range" are visible through the windows of the boarding house across from Coverdale's hotel. The blue is picked up again in the blue spectacles which a pale man wore at the village-hall. When Coverdale returns to Blithedale after his vacation in the city, he observes the green of the trees; the "crimson and gold" of those which have turned early; the scarlet fruit; the "orchards of ruddy apples, and fields of ripening maize"; the toadstools, "some spotlessly white, others yellow or red"; and finally the greensward, the red clay, and the deep-purple grapes of the farm. In his description of the masquerade party, Hawthorne uses few color-adjectives, but he suggests the variety of hues in the masquers' costumes: an Indian chief with his war paint; the goddess Diana; a Bavarian broom girl; a Kentucky woodsman; a Shaker elder and grim Puritans, for contrast; Shepherds of Arcadia; figures from the *Faerie Queene;* gay Cavaliers and Revolutionary officers; a "bright complexioned, dark-haired, vivacious little gypsy, with a red shawl over her head"; "Moll Pitcher, the renowned old witch of Lynn"; Silas Porter in his customary blue suit; "some old-fashioned skinkers and drawers, all with portentously red noses"; and a "horned and long-tailed gentleman." Finally, just before her death, Zenobia speaks of Priscilla who will "make as soft and gentle a wife as the veriest Bluebeard could desire," a prophetic culmination of the blue sequence. Although there are no references in the novel to the color of Zenobia's flower, we picture it as bright red or scarlet, perhaps because it is tropical and rare and also, undoubtedly, because of Zenobia's black hair.

When I think of Hawthorne's novels in terms of color, I think of *The House of the Seven Gables* as being a dull yellow and green, almost brown—whereas *The Scarlet Letter* is red and black.[4] An analysis of color in *Seven Gables* supports this subjective reaction. Suprisingly, however, the color most frequently mentioned is red (including crimson and scarlet). But this is Hawthorne; he cannot resist spots of red. The color next in frequency is gold. Yellow and green tie for third place, with blue and brown next in order. The word *purple,* I believe, is used only once. Leaving out the red, which somehow has very little weight, we could mix all the other pigments together in the proportion given and get the yellowish-greenish-brown, with highlights and shadows, which the novel seems to have. Here again, Hawthorne's impressionistic technique appears. He puts spots of color on the canvas and lets the observer's eye do the mixing. This he has certainly done in *Seven Gables.* We also note with interest that most of the color in this novel is in the quiet middle part where it is needed. Less than a sixth of the color references are in the last part where emotional tension is great without the aid of objective devices.

In *The Marble Faun,* although the color most often mentioned is red, the color that is dominant and that gives brilliancy to the story is gold: the golden sunshine of Italy, the gold of many altars, the golden glory of Rome, and the golden glow of Monte Beni's famous wine, Sunshine. With a true feeling for chiaroscuro, Hawthorne often mentions brown and yellow, the shadows and highlights of the gold. With his usual sense of the value of contrast, the two colors he most frequently mentions (aside from red and gold) are blue and purple. As in *The Blithedale Romance,* there is a scene of particular gayety, with masquers in brilliant costumes: "Fantastic figures, with bulbous heads"; Harlequins; a "little, long-tailed, horned fiend"; a "biped, with an ass's

---

[4] "*The House of the Seven Gables* is the Romance of Heredity. The colors are gray and sombre, with some pretty fantastic detail in pale rose and green where Phoebe's tender girlishness or womanliness appears."—Lewis E. Gates, *Studies and Appreciations* (New York, Macmillan Company, 1900), p. 97.

snout"; "a clown in motley"; "clowns and parti-colored harlequins"; "bear-headed, bull-headed, and dog-headed individuals"; "quaint figures, in the stately ruff, the cloak, tunic, and trunk-hose, of three centuries ago"; and many other fantastic and colorful costumes.

Sombre tones color "The Minister's Black Veil." To list samples of the images which contribute to these tones is unnecessary. The many references to the black veil itself give "a darkened aspect to all living and inanimate things." Even Mr. Hooper's sermons are "tinged, rather more darkly than usual, with the gentle gloom of Mr. Hooper's temperament." All through the story are gloomy but sedate references to things of death and darkness. The picture is unquestionably black. But an entirely black picture would not be visible. There must be some light to give shape to objects. There must be differences in tone to give interest to the picture. Hawthorne gives us light, and variations in tone, and even a few spots of color. To contrast immediately with the black and to help outline the objects are a few spots of white: the starched band of the clergyman's costume; the oldest parishioner, "a white-haired great-grandsire"; the maiden's spirit which might be walking hand in hand with the minister; the bride's "deathlike paleness"; the minister's own lips that grew white when he caught sight of himself in a mirror; the years which had shed "their snows above his sable veil"; and the "hoary head of good Father Hooper upon the death-pillow." These spots of white are not accidental. Hawthorne could quite easily have avoided using them if he had wished. If he did not deliberately plant them at regular intervals throughout the story, he might have done so, and he certainly did use them consciously. Just as occasional accelerations in tempo relieve and accent the slow movement of this story, so these spots of white relieve and accent the black. Similarly, a few spots of warm color, often red or suggestive of red, enliven and give variety to the sombre tones. Shining through the blackness are such phrases as "the midnight

lamp," "the light of the candles," "a glass of wine," "a cheerful gleam from the hearth," "the color rose into her cheeks,"
"at sunset," and "shaded candlelight." The word *crime*, frequently used, certainly suggests some color, if not a definite
red. And finally, at the very end of the story, Hawthorne
writes:

> Still veiled, they laid him in his coffin, and a veiled corpse
> they bore him to his grave. The grass of many years has
> sprung up and withered on that grave, the burial stone is
> moss-grown . . . [I, 62-63]

Here are two suggestions of green. They are the *only* color
except red used in the entire story, and quite appropriately,
they are in direct contrast to red.

Black and white is the scheme of "Edward Randolph's
Portrait." The portrait in the story is all black, so black that
the features cannot be distinguished. It is mounted in an
ebony frame. When Alice Vane, by art or magic, reveals it in
its original form for the inspiration of Lieutenant-Governor
Hutchinson its blackness is accented by the implied white of
the figure's ruff:

> Within the antique frame, which so recently had enclosed
> a sable waste of canvas, now appeared a visible picture, still
> dark, indeed, in its hues and shadings, but thrown forward
> in strong relief. It was a half-length figure of a gentleman in
> a rich, but very old-fashioned dress of embroidered velvet,
> with a broad ruff and a beard, and wearing a hat, the brim
> of which overshadowed his forehead. Beneath this cloud
> the eyes had a peculiar glare which was almost lifelike.
> The whole portrait started so distinctly out of the back-
> ground, that it had the effect of a person looking down from
> the wall at the astonished and awe-stricken spectators. [II,
> 41-42]

This spot of white, the broad ruff, is pointed up in advance
by the author's reference to Alice Vane: "She was clad entirely in white, a pale, ethereal creature." [II, 30] This appears
very early in the narrative. Shortly before the revelation of
the portrait, we find three more spots of white: the members

of the council "dressed in white wigs"; "a branched silver candlestick, throwing down the glow of half a dozen wax-lights upon a paper apparently ready for the Lieutenant-Governor's signature"; [II, 37] and another mention of "the white drapery of a lady's robe." [II, 38] Just before Hutchinson signs the document, Edward Randolph's portrait is revealed. In spite of his momentary fear, Hutchinson "scrawled on the paper, in characters that betokened it a deed of desperation, the name of Thomas Hutchinson." [II, 43] The black signature on the white paper, paper made all the more white by the glare of candlelight upon it! The frame of this story repeats and emphasizes the scheme of the narrative within the frame. Like the frames of all the legends of the Province House, it deals with the old house, Haw-thorne's visit there, and Mr. Bela Tiffany's story. The house and the room are as dark as the ebony frame of the portrait. In this surrounding structure Hawthorne includes his usual spot of red, "a dark stratum of port wine" in the whisky-punch, and this color is repeated by two or three references to blood within the narrative itself. At the end of the story, Hawthorne writes: ". . . I took leave of the circle round the fireside of the Province House, and plunging down the door-steps, fought my way homeward against a drifting snow-storm." [II, 45] At the beginning of the story he tells us that he made his second visit to the Province House in January. Although he describes the night as "chill and raw, and rendered boisterous by almost a gale of wind," he does not mention the snow. It is only when he leaves the house that he refers to it. There seems to be no occasion to bring in the snow at the end of the story except for the purpose of repeating, and thereby stressing, the black and white.

Amid the black and white of "The White Old Maid" are to be found two or three spots of color. As in "The Minister's Black Veil" there is a reference to the green of graves. This is the first touch of color in the story. The last touch is again green: "a lock of hair, once sable, now discolored with a

greenish mould." [II, 202] The only other color reference is
to a "red gleam" which shows out of the darkness of the old
house. [II, 198] This spot of red is approximately midway
between the two green spots. Hawthorne often uses color
with as much care for design as a first-rate painter. "Ethan
Brand" is another story done in black and white with the
usual touch of red. There is the black of the night and the
charcoal, the white of marble and lime, and the red of the
kiln's "lurid blaze." At the end of the story, the sunlight's
"gold upon the mountain tops" is an added accent and a
pleasing contrast. There are very few other colors, and they
are largely descriptive: Ethan's brown clothes, Lawyer Giles'
purple face, and the occasional blue tips of the flame.

The small red hand in "The Birthmark" is a fine example
of Hawthorne's devotion to red symbols. Except for the red,
this story is not very colorful. We have already noted the
brilliant contrasts in "The Birthmark," and, of course, such
contrasts indirectly lend color to a story. There is a touch
of blue here, and an "empurpled radiance," but for the most
part the story is pictured in dark, sombre tones relieved only
by red. Hawthorne makes the red hand more vibrant by
setting it off against different backgrounds:

> In the usual state of her complexion—a healthy though
> delicate bloom—the mark wore a tint of deeper crimson,
> which imperfectly defined its shape amid the surrounding
> rosiness. When she blushed it gradually became more in-
> distinct, and finally vanished amid the triumphant rush of
> blood that bathed the whole cheek with its brilliant glow.
> But if any shifting emotion caused her to turn pale, there
> was the mark again, a crimson stain upon the snow, in what
> Aylmer sometimes deemed an almost fearful distinctness.
> [IV, 50]

The red birthmark is first shown in its faint normal appearance. Then it is made to disappear against the ruddiness
of Georgianna's blush. Finally it is shown in its most brilliant state against her pale face. Hawthorne has chosen
exactly the right order in which to present these images. Had

he reversed or changed the order, the passage would have lost some of its impressiveness. References to the birthmark and its redness appear often and in many forms in this story.

The little spot of red, as we have noted, appears in one way or another in many of Hawthorne's tales. In "Chippings with a Chisel" the favorite color takes the form of allusions to a rose. There is first the "rose hanging its head from a broken stem" which Mr. Wigglesworth carves on the seaman's stone; then there is the woman "with a pretty rosebud of a daughter"; and finally there is a girl, "a pale, slender, feeble creature, most unlike the other rosy and healthful damsels of the Vineyard." The ever-present spot of red appears in "Feathertop" as the glow of Mother Rigby's pipe. In "My Kinsman, Major Molineux" there is the red petticoat of the girl who tries to waylay Robin, the red and black face of the strange man, and the red light of torches illuminating Major Molineux's disgrace. These flashes of color, incidentally, prefigure the outcome and help hold the two parts of the story together. And there is, it almost goes without saying, the scarlet letter, which shall be discussed at some length later.

Hawthorne is adept at painting pictures in black and white so that they have a silver glow. He is skilful with high-lights and shadows. In "Dr. Heidegger's Experiment" we read about the scientist's marvelous liquid:

> It was apparently impregnated with an effervescent gas, for little bubbles were continually ascending from the depths of the glasses, and bursting in silvery spray at the surface. [I, 313]

In *The House of the Seven Gables* we read of the refreshing contrast between the heat of the day and the cool of the evening:

> So sweetly cool was the atmosphere, after all the feverish day, that the summer eve might be fancied as sprinkling dews and liquid moonlight, with a dash of icy temper in them, out of a silver vase. [VII, 310-11]

The last two words of this sentence give color to the atmos-
phere and the evening as well as to the dew and the moonlight. Moonlight, or starlight, of course, offers a splendid
subject for such pictures. The light of the moon often pene-
trates the Pyncheon house and high-lights moments of
intense emotion. Throughout the chapter entitled "Governor
Pyncheon," where Jaffray sits motionless in the Colonel's
chair, the moon and stars are important though faint sources
of illumination:

> The northwest wind has swept the sky clear. The window is
> distinctly seen. Through its panes, moreover, we dimly catch
> the sweep of the dark, clustering foliage outside, fluttering
> with a constant irregularity of movement, and letting in a
> peep of starlight, now here, now there. Oftener than any
> other object, these glimpses illuminate the Judge's face. But
> here comes more effectual light. Observe that silvery dance
> upon the upper branches of the pear-tree, and now a little
> lower, and now on the whole mass of boughs, while, through
> their shifting intricacies, the moonbeams fall aslant into the
> room. They play over the Judge's figure and show that he
> has not stirred throughout the hours of darkness. They
> follow the shadows, in changeful sport, across his unchang-
> ing features. They gleam upon his watch. [VII, 405]

With spots of silver light, the greater for the contrasting
darkness, Hawthorne produces an intriguing picture in black
and white. There are many such pictures in *Seven Gables* as
well as in the other stories.

F. O. Matthiessen speaks of Hawthorne's "way of developing his plot by means of a few spot-lighted scenes."[5] We can
find ample evidence to support the idea. We see this spot-
lighting in "The Artist of the Beautiful," "The Haunted
Mind," "The Ambitious Guest," and in many other tales.
Rarely is this device more apparent or more suitable than in
"The Vision of the Fountain." Twice Hawthorne sees the
vision. The first time it is at the fountain where a "solitary
sunbeam found its way down, and played like a goldfish in

---

[5] *American Renaissance* (New York, Oxford University Press, 1941), p. 203.

the water." The author looks into the fountain for the "Naiad of the spring" which his youth tells him must be there:

> I looked again, and lo! another face, deeper in the fountain than my own image, more distinct in all the features, yet faint as thought. The vision had the aspect of a fair young girl, with locks of paly gold. . . . The solitary sunbeam was diffused among the golden hair, which melted into its faint brightness, and became a glory round that head so beautiful!
>
> My description can give no idea how suddenly the fountain was thus tenanted, and how soon it was left desolate. I breathed, and there was the face! I held my breath, and it was gone. [1, 288-89]

The second time he sees the vision, it is in the Squire's parlor, and then "there was no light, except the little that came sullenly from two half-burned brands, without even glimmering on the andirons." He hears a voice which has a vaguely familiar tone:

> Suddenly the dry pine caught; the fire blazed up with a ruddy glow; and where the darkness had been, there was she—the Vision of the Fountain! A spirit of radiance only, she had vanished with the rainbow, and appeared again in the firelight, perhaps to flicker with the blaze, and be gone. Yet, her cheek was rosy and lifelike, and her features, in the bright warmth of the room, were even sweeter and tenderer than my recollection of them. She knew me! The mirthful expression that had laughed in her eyes and dimpled over her countenance, when I beheld her faint beauty in the fountain, was laughing and dimpling there now. One moment our glance mingled—the next, down rolled the heap of tan upon the kindled wood—and darkness snatched away that Daughter of the Light, and gave her back to me no more! [1, 295]

Hawthorne can never be accused of lacking variety in his design. In the first appearance of the vision, the sunlight is constant and the girl moves away; in the second appearance, the girl does not move but the firelight flares up and then dies down again. Another difference between the two passages is that of the texture and color of the light. The vision

first appears in a clear, golden, crystalline light; she appears
the second time in an unsteady, cloudy, ruddy glow. The two
high points of the story are spotted by intense lights.

Spots of light, woven into a rhythmic motif, emphasize
the principal scenes in "The Wives of the Dead." In no other
short story does Hawthorne depend so much on light and
use it to such good advantage. It is like a picture drawn
with glowing colors on black paper. The story begins on the
"rainy twilight of an autumn day" and, in their parlor, two
young women sit together by the fireside. After they have
eaten their dinner on a "table before the fire," they go to
their respective rooms:

> Thither the widowed ones retired, after heaping ashes upon
> the dying embers of their fire, and placing a lighted lamp
> upon the hearth. The doors of both chambers were left open,
> so that a part of the interior of each, and the beds, with their
> unclosed curtains, were reciprocally visible. [III, 272]

Hawthorne economically uses the lamp on the hearth to
illuminate the two bedrooms and the parlor, all at the same
time:

> The cold light of the lamp threw the shadows of the furni-
> ture up against the wall, stamping them immovably there,
> except when they were shaken by a sudden flicker of the
> flame. Two vacant armchairs were in their old positions on
> opposite sides of the hearth, where the brothers had been
> wont to sit in young and laughing dignity, as heads of
> families . . . The cheerful radiance of the fire had shone
> upon the happy circle, and the dead glimmer of the lamp
> might have befitted their reunion now. [III, 273]

A knock at the outside door suddenly draws Margaret out
of her peaceful sleep and her revery:

> Seizing the lamp from the hearth, she hastened to the
> window that overlooked the street-door. It was a lattice,
> turning upon hinges; and having thrown it back, she
> stretched her head a little way into the moist atmosphere.
> A lantern was reddening the front of the house, and melting
> its light in the neighboring puddles, while a deluge of dark-

ness overwhelmed every other object. As the window grated
on its hinges, a man in a broad-brimmed hat and blanket
coat stepped from under the shelter of the projecting story ...
[III, 274]

Margaret talks with this man and learns that her husband is
not dead, but has just been seen alive:

> So saying, the honest man departed; and his lantern
> gleamed along the street, bringing to view indistinct shapes
> of things, and the fragments of a world, like order gleaming
> through chaos, or memory roaming over the past. But
> Margaret stayed not to watch these picturesque effects.
> [III, 275-76]

No sooner has Margaret gone to bed again than Mary, the
other widowed girl, has a similar experience. She too, in the
midst of her half-sleep, hears a knock at the door:

> At the same moment, the pang of recollection darted into
> her mind; the pall of sleep was thrown back from the face
> of grief; the dim light of the chamber, and the objects
> therein revealed, had retained all her suspended ideas, and
> restored them as soon as she unclosed her eyes. Again
> there was a quick peal upon the street door. Fearing that
> her sister would also be disturbed, Mary wrapped herself in
> a cloak and hood, took the lamp from the hearth, and
> hastened to the window. [III, 277]

Like Margaret, Mary opens the window and finds a mes-
senger waiting for her:

> The storm was over, and the moon was up; it shone upon
> broken clouds above, and below upon houses black with
> moisture, and upon little lakes of the fallen rain, curling
> into silver beneath the quick enchantment of a breeze. A
> young man in a sailor's dress, wet as if he had come out
> of the depths of the sea, stood alone under the window.
> [III, 278]

This young man leaves his message—that Mary's husband
is still alive—and departs:

> He hurried away, while Mary watched him with a doubt
> of waking reality, that seemed stronger or weaker as he

alternately entered the shade of the houses, or emerged into
the broad streaks of moonlight. [III, 279]

Hawthorne implies, in the last word of the story, that both
of these incidents are probably dreams. There is certainly
a dream-like quality about the lights and shadows in the
picture which are both sharp and at the same time vague, as
in dreams. The story is very short, scarcely seven pages. The
above passages have been quoted at some length to show the
large proportion of the tale devoted to spot-lighted scenes.
Although "The Wives of the Dead" is exceptional, many of
Hawthorne's tales present pictures which are seen in the light
of lamps or fires or in strong sunlight or moonlight. "John
Inglefield's Thanksgiving" takes place in a room lighted
by an open fire. "Earth's Holocaust" and "The Devil in
Manuscript" glow with fire-light. "Young Goodman Brown"
and "Ethan Brand" depend largely on fire-light for their
illumination. This, I suppose, is a typically romantic element
in Hawthorne's writing.

Hawthorne makes much less use of sound than many
writers do. His auditory imagination may have been weak
or undeveloped. There is no evidence of any great love for
or appreciation of music,[6] although he exclaims in *Seven
Gables,* "What an instrument is the human voice!" [VII, 136]
When he thinks of sound, it is often in terms of color. As
we noted before, he asks: "Can the tolling of the Old South
bell be painted?" He speaks of Hepzibah Pyncheon's voice
as having been "dyed black," or as being "like a black silken
thread, on which the crystal beads of speech are strung, and
whence they take their hue." [VII, 193-94] Elsewhere, he
comments that if cities were built to the tune of music,
"edifices would appear to be constructed by grave, solemn
tones," or by "light, fantastic airs." He apparently sees sound.

---

[6] Julian Hawthorne speaks of his father's "insensibility to music—he was wont
to declare that he could never distinguish between 'Yankee Doodle' and 'Hail
Columbia.' "—*Nathaniel Hawthorne and his Wife* (Boston, James R. Osgood and
Co., 1885), I, 103.

We cannot deny, however, that he quite often achieves sound-images and sound-patterns of considerable effectiveness. Sometimes his sound "pictures" are largely in black and white, as this one from "The Ambitious Guest":

> But the family were glad again when they perceived that the latch was lifted by some traveller, whose footsteps had been unheard amid the dreary blast which heralded his approach, and wailed as he was entering, and went moaning away from the door. [II, 122]

Sometimes sound is colorful, as in a passage from "The Haunted Mind":

> The distant sound of a church clock is borne faintly on the wind. You question with yourself, half seriously, whether it has stolen to your waking ear from some gray tower that stood within the precincts of your dream. While yet in suspense, another clock flings its heavy clang over the slumbering town, with so full and distinct a sound, and such a long murmur in the neighboring air, that you are certain it must proceed from the steeple at the nearest corner. You count the strokes—one—two, and there they cease, with a booming sound, like the gathering of a third stroke within the bell. [II, 93-94]

A lively series of sounds can be heard in a paragraph from "The Toll-Gatherer's Day":

> In the morning—dim, gray, dewy summer's morn—the distant roll of ponderous wheels begins to mingle with my old friend's slumbers, creaking more and more harshly through the midst of his dream, and gradually replacing it with realities. Hardly conscious of the change from sleep to wakefulness, he finds himself partly clad and throwing wide the toll-gates for the passage of a fragrant load of hay. The timbers groan beneath the slow-revolving wheels; one sturdy yeoman stalks beside the oxen, and, peering from the summit of the hay, by the glimmer of the half-extinguished lantern over the toll-house, is seen the drowsy visage of his comrade, who has enjoyed a nap some ten miles long. The toll is paid—creak, creak, again go the wheels, and the huge haymow vanishes into the morning mist. As yet nature is

but half awake, and familiar objects appear visionary. But yonder, dashing from the shore with a rattling thunder of the wheels and a confused clatter of hoofs, comes the never-tiring mail, which has hurried onward at the same headlong, restless rate, all through the quiet night. The bridge resounds in one continued peal as the coach rolls on without a pause, merely affording the toll-gatherer a glimpse at the sleepy passengers, who now bestir their torpid limbs and snuff a cordial in the briny air. [1, 278-79]

We hear the soft, blurred "distant roll" of sound. Then we hear the groaning of the bridge under retarding wheels and the accelerated creaking of wheels that are starting to roll again. As this sound diminishes into the distance, a sudden and violent crescendo occurs. It is not the slowly increasing volume of the haymow rumble but the quick, brief, bursting roar of the mail as it rushes by. This sound is amplified by the resonance of the bridge which seems to reverberate even after the coach has passed by. Then Hawthorne adds, for emphasis by contrast, the quiet sounds of "sleepy passengers, who now bestir their torpid limbs." These sounds are designed to make audible the awakening of the world on a summer morning. As a means to that end, they are a clever device. Standing alone, as a design in sound, they evoke sharp auditory images.

The sound-pattern of "Young Goodman Brown" begins when the old woman, Goody Cloyse, recognizes Goodman Brown's strange companion: "'The devil!' screamed the pious old lady." Goody Cloyse disappears and so does the devil, and the Goodman is left alone in the forest. From this point on, the various sound images are frequent and intense. It will be worthwhile to take them out of their context in order to hear them:

On came the hoof tramps and the voices of the riders, two grave old voices, conversing soberly as they drew near. These mingled sounds appeared to pass along the road, within a few yards of the young man's hiding-place; but owing, doubtless, to the depth of the gloom at that particular spot, neither the travellers nor their steeds were visible. [IV, 112]

The hoofs clattered again; and the voices, talking so strangely in the empty air, passed on through the forest, where no church had ever been gathered or solitary Christian prayed. [IV, 113]

Aloft in the air, as if from the depths of the cloud, came a confused and doubtful sound of voices. Once the listener fancied that he could distinguish the accents of town's-people of his own, men and women both pious and ungodly, many of whom he had met at the communion-table, and had seen others rioting at the tavern. The next moment, so indistinct were the sounds, he doubted whether he had heard aught but the murmur of the old forest, whispering without a wind. Then came a stronger swell of those familiar tones, heard daily in the sunshine at Salem village, but never until now from a cloud of night. There was one voice, of a young woman, uttering lamentations, yet with an uncertain sorrow, and entreating for some favor, which, perhaps, it would grieve her to obtain. And all the unseen multitude, both saints and sinners, seemed to encourage her onward.

"Faith!" shouted Goodman Brown, in a voice of agony and desperation; and the echoes of the forest mocked him, crying—"Faith! Faith!" as if bewildered wretches were seeking her all through the wilderness.

The cry of grief, rage, and terror was yet piercing the night, when the unhappy husband held his breath for a response. There was a scream, drowned immediately in a louder murmur of voices, fading into far-off laughter, as the dark cloud swept away, leaving the clear and silent sky above Goodman Brown. [IV, 114-15]

The whole forest was peopled with frightful sounds—the creaking of the trees, the howling of wild beasts, and the yell of Indians; while sometimes the wind tolled like a distant church bell, and sometimes gave a broad roar around the traveller, as if all Nature were laughing him to scorn. [IV, 115]

"Ha! ha! ha!" roared Goodman Brown when the wind laughed at him. "Let us hear which will laugh loudest. Think not to frighten me with your deviltry. Come witch, come wizard, come Indian powwow, come devil himself! and here comes Goodman Brown." [IV, 115-16]

On he flew among the black pines, brandishing his staff with frenzied gestures, now giving vent to an inspiration of horrid blasphemy, and now shouting forth such laughter as set all the echoes of the forest laughing like demons around him. . . . He paused, in a lull of the tempest that had driven him onward, and heard the swell of what seemed a hymn, rolling solemnly from a distance with the weight of many voices. He knew the tune; it was a familiar one in the choir of the village meeting-house. The verse died heavily away, and was lengthened by a chorus, not of human voices, but of all the sounds of the benighted wilderness pealing in awful harmony together. Goodman Brown cried out, and his cry was lost to his own ear by its unison with the cry of the desert. [IV, 116-17]

Another verse of the hymn arose, a slow and mournful strain, such as the pious love, but joined to words which expressed all that our nature can conceive of sin, and darkly hinted at far more. Unfathomable to mere mortals is the lore of fiends. Verse after verse was sung; and still the chorus of the desert swelled between like the deepest tone of a mighty organ; and with the final peal of that dreadful anthem there came a sound, as if the roaring wind, the rushing streams, the howling beasts, and every other voice of the unconcerted wilderness were mingling and according with the voice of guilty man in homage to the prince of all. [IV, 118-19]

"Bring forth the converts!" cried a voice that echoed through the field and rolled into the forest. [IV, 119]

"Welcome," repeated the fiend-worshippers, in one cry of despair and triumph. [IV, 122]

"Faith! Faith!" cried the husband. "Look up to heaven, and resist the wicked one."
Whether Faith obeyed he knew not. Hardly had he spoken when he found himself amid calm night and solitude, listening to a roar of the wind which died heavily away through the forest. [IV, 122-23]

These passages speak for themselves. The sound-composition, thus isolated, makes an interesting pattern. Hoof-beats and voices; more voices; murmuring of the wind; a woman's sorrowful lamentation; Goodman Brown's shout; the forest's echo; a scream; laughter; silence. Creaking and howling; distant church bells; laughter; more laughter; silence. A hymn sung by many voices; the young man's outcry; the hymn again; a strong, rolling voice; a triumphant echo; Goodman Brown's cry of desperation; the murmuring of the forest; silence. Very few writers and not many musicians could compose such music. There is harmony and melody. There is rhythm and counterpoint, and there are solo voices. It is like a magnificent orchestration; it is like the last movement of Beethoven's Ninth Symphony. Of course, it is true that all this music is scattered through the story. The reader does not hear it as a whole. But its effect is still felt and it unifies and dominates the account of Goodman Brown. It is the musical background for his dream.

Laughter also rolls through "Ethan Brand"—in seven long waves. We hear it in the first paragraph: "a roar of laughter, not mirthful, but slow, and even solemn, like a wind shaking the boughs of a forest." [III, 112] We hear it again when Bartram, "with a laugh," questions Ethan Brand: this is a small, uncertain, chilled laugh. [III, 118] After a few pages, Ethan laughs again; and Hawthorne comments on laughter:

> It was the same slow, heavy laugh that almost appalled the lime-burner when it heralded the wayfarer's approach.
> The solitary mountain-side was made dismal by it. Laughter, when out of place, mistimed, or bursting forth from a disordered state of feeling, may be the most terrible modulation of the human voice. The laughter of one asleep, even if it be a little child,—the madman's laugh,—the wild, screaming laugh of a born idiot,—are sounds that we sometimes tremble to hear, and would always willingly forget. Poets have imagined no utterance of fiends or hobgobblins so fearfully appropriate as a laugh. And even the obtuse lime-burner felt his nerves shaken, as this strange man looked inward at his own heart, and burst into laughter that rolled away into the night, and was indistinctly reverberated among the hills. [III, 118-19]

We note that Hawthorne does not mention the gay and joyous laughter that warms the heart of all who hear it. He is, of course, not writing an essay on laughter, but rather giving color to Ethan's "slow, heavy laugh" by suggesting the sleeper's and the madman's and the idiot's laugh. He is filling-out the tone. The fourth laugh is that of the villagers who come to look at Ethan. They are laughing "boisterously, and mingling all their voices together in unceremonious talk." [III, 123] Then, after a pause of several pages, we hear the cheerful "universal laughter, clapping of hands, and shouts of encore" [III, 132] in response to the stray dog's antics. This is followed immediately by another single laugh, Ethan Brand's again:

> . . . he broke into the awful laugh which, more than any other token, expressed the condition of his inward being. From that moment, the merriment of the party was at an end; they stood aghast, dreading lest the inauspicious sound should be reverberated around the horizon, and that mountain would thunder it to mountain, and so the horror be prolonged upon their ears. [III, 132-33]

The awfulness of Ethan's laughter is increased—somewhat negatively—by reference to possible reverberation, and its horror is augmented by the suggestion that it is big enough to be thundered from mountain to mountain. Finally, we hear "the sound of a fearful peal of laughter" which "rolled heavily through the sleep of the lime-burner and his little son." [III, 137] How much more fearful this laughter than if it were heard by listeners who were awake! In spite of his description of idiot's laughs and laughs which reverberate among the hills, Hawthorne has saved the most horrible for this last one—Ethan's last. We may use such a term as *understatement* to describe this, but what we really mean is artistry through selection, rhythm, and contrast. Here is a sound pattern the more effective because it is in opposition to the general temper of the story. There can be no doubt that Hawthorne planned to use laughter for an emotional effect, and that he distributed and arranged the laughs in just this particular pattern intentionally. His brief general discussion of laughter calls attention to his pattern, just as he probably intended it to do.

The sound in "Rappaccini's Daughter" is well worth noting. The first sound is the gushing of the fountain in the midst of the garden, "a little gurgling sound . . . that sung its song unceasingly." Then Giovanni "heard a rustling sound." Soon he hears Beatrice call to her father in a "rich and youthful voice . . . a voice as rich as a tropical sunset." Again she speaks in "rich tones," and again "with her rich voice, that came forth as it were like a gush of music." Later we hear "the sound of rustling leaves," and "the rustling of a silken garment." Beatrice speaks "with the music of a pleasant laugh." Then, when Giovanni reaches for the poison flower, "Beatrice darted forward, uttering a shriek that went through his heart like a dagger." Again Beatrice "sent up the rich sweetness of her tones to float around him in his chamber and echo and reverberate through his heart." After Baglioni tells him of the horrors of Rappaccini's scientific investigation, "Giovanni groaned and hid his face." Once more "a rich, sweet voice came floating up from the garden." Later, " 'Accursed one!' cried he, with venomous scorn." And Beatrice murmured "with a low moan out of her heart." Then she spoke "calmly," and then she "shrieked." As she was dying, she spoke "feebly" and finally "murmured." Hawthorne varies the intensity and quality and pitch of sounds in this story. In the first half of the tale, the sounds are chiefly those of nature, gurgling, rustling sounds, intermingled with the clear, high, soft notes of Beatrice's voice. Then they shift to the lower, harsher sounds of human emotions. We cannot help noticing how Beatrice's shriek stands out against the more quiet and harmonious tones. It is also notable that the sounds in "Rappaccini's Daughter" support the vibrating movement and color which has been so apparent. Hawthorne does not often use sound to any large extent in his tales, but when he does, he uses it well. The sound-imagery in *The Marble Faun* is disappointing. It promises, in the early parts of the novel, to be patterned and colorful; but it dwindles off. It lacks the continuity which we shall find in *The House of the Seven Gables* and is much less effective than the sound-pattern in several of the short stories. Near the beginning, we hear the four-part harmony of the alarm when Miriam's friends call for her in the catacombs: "Kenyon with his bass voice; Donatello with his tenor; the guide with that high and hard Italian cry . . .; and Hilda with her slender scream." We can hear the gay music in the garden of the Villa Borghese, "comprising a harp, a flute, and a violin." On the Pincian, we can hear the French military band which "flings out rich music over the poor old city, floating her with strains as loud as those of her own echoless triumphs," and the church bell which rings out "as if it were a peal of triumph because Rome is still imperial." We can hear, also, the noise of falling water from the Fountain of Trevi; "scraps of songs, with much laughter and merriment between the stanzas"; songs which are sung in the moonlight; Miriam's "loud, fearful cry, which quivered upward through the air, and sank quivering down to the earth," as the model is killed; and the "deep, lugubrious strain of a *De Profundis,* which sounded like an utterance of the tomb itself," at the model's funeral. In Book Two, we hear, at Monte Beni, wandering musicians who make "the lawn and shrubbery tuneful with the sound of fiddle, harp, and flute, and now and then with the tangled squeaking of a bagpipe"; Donatello's "wild, rude, yet harmonious" cries as he calls the nymph; the convent-bell which "was not only echoed among the hills, but answered by another bell, and still another"; the low, sad strain of a woman's voice somewhere in the old castle; and the market-music at Perugia, an organ-grinder, a clarion, and a flute. This is all. The sounds are interesting, vivid, and effective in themselves, but they are unrelated. We are disappointed because we have hoped for more, and these sounds could so easily have been woven into an expressive pattern throughout the novel.

Neither does there seem to be a clear-cut pattern of sound in *The House of the Seven Gables,* but here the sounds are somewhat related, and several sound-sequences carry through the book. The shop-bell tinkles on and off. Its tones, though melodically agreeable, are not pleasing to the residents of the house. Hepzibah dislikes the sound because it is a reminder of the commercial activity which she despises and for which she is so unsuited; Clifford, calling it "a hateful clamor," finds it disturbing to his sensitive soul. However, if any sound may be considered the audible expression of *Seven Gable's* moral, it is the shop-bell. Alice's harpsichord, actually heard only once, is another sound-motif. We are often told about it, and each mention of the instrument carries with it penetrating connotations.

The house itself has many of the queer sounds which old houses, at least in literature, always have. These sounds are all gathered together and amplified on the stormy night when the dead Jaffray sits alone in the house:

> But, listen! That puff of breeze was louder; it had a tone unlike the dreary and sullen one which has bemoaned itself, and afflicted all mankind with miserable sympathy, for five days past. The wind has veered about! It now comes boisterously from the northwest, and, taking hold of the aged framework of the Seven Gables, gives it a shake, like a wrestler that would try strength with his antagonist. Another and another sturdy tussle with the blast! The old house creaks again, and makes a vociferous but somewhat unintelligible bellowing in its sooty throat (the big flue, we mean, of its wide chimney), partly in complaint at the rude wind, but rather, as befits their century and a half of hostile intimacy, in tough defiance. A rumbling kind of a bluster roars behind the fire-board. A door has slammed above stairs. A window, perhaps, has been left open, or else is driven in by an unruly gust. It is not to be conceived, beforehand, what wonderful wind-instruments are these old timber mansions, and how haunted with the strangest

noises, which immediately begin to sing, and sigh, and sob, and shriek,—and to smite with sledge-hammers, airy but ponderous in some distant chamber,—and to tread along the entries as with stately footsteps, and rustle up and down the staircase, as with silks miraculously stiff,—whenever the gale catches the house with a window open, and gets fairly into it. Would that we **were** not an attendant spirit here! It is too awful! This clamor of the wind through the lonely house; the Judge's quietude, as he sits invisible; and that pertinacious ticking of his watch! [vii, 403-405]

The last sentence, bringing in the rhythmic sound of the watch and Jaffray's silence, by way of contrast, is a fine summary and an excellent conclusion to the paragraph. Although there are several sound-words, such as *louder, creaks, bellowing, sing, sigh, rustle,* and so on, the effect of this sound "picture" lies mostly in its suggestiveness. Hawthorne describes the wind and lets the reader, for the most part, supply his own sound accompaniment.

There are several other good bits of sound-imagery. In chapter six, Phoebe hears "the murmur of an unknown voice" three times on the night before Clifford's arrival. The first time it is "strangly indistinct . . . and less like articulate words than an unshaped sound." The second time it is "an irregular respiration in some obscure corner of the room." And the third time, while Phoebe is in bed, it is a "strange, vague murmur, which might be likened to an indistinct shadow of human utterance." It is not alone by describing sounds, by saying that they are "strangely indistinct" or that a voice spoke "with a hush through it" that Hawthorne stimulates sound-images in his readers' minds. He relies on auxiliary effects and personal reactions. In connection with the above unknown voice, he tells us that Phoebe "sat silently for a moment," and then, "her senses being very acute," she is able to locate the sound more accurately. Perhaps empathy enters in at this point. In any case, by the breathless pause which is suggested, our own experience comes into play and sharpens our hearing. When we read that the sound was so vague that "its impression or echo in Phoebe's mind was that of unreality," we feel something of her reaction to the sound. Here, as in all his best writing, Hawthorne builds up a stimulus out of varied materials, a stimulus which results in a striking image in the reader's mind. The parade and the barrel-organ, heard through the arched window, are small but colorful spots of sound. They are heard in the middle chapter of the book. In this same chapter we hear another sound which is related, by contrast, to the shop-bell:

> The church-bells, with various tones, but all in harmony, were calling out and responding to one another,—"It is the Sabbath!—the Sabbath!—Yea; the Sabbath!"—and over the whole city the bells scattered the blessed sounds, now slowly, now with livelier joy, now one bell alone, now all the bells together, crying earnestly,—"It is the Sabbath!" and flinging their accents afar off, to melt into the air, and pervade it with the holy word. [VII, 241]

Melody, harmony, rhythm, and intense feeling—all that any music can ever have—is found in the ringing of these bells. This chapter, eleven, has more sound than any other in the book. It is a refreshing oasis in the exact middle of a relatively quiet novel.

A passage from *The Blithedale Romance* is about as inclusive as any passage could be in its array of sounds:

> Whatever had been my taste for solitude and natural scenery, yet the thick, foggy, stifled element of cities, the entangled life of many men together, sordid as it was, and empty of the beautiful, took quite as strenuous a hold upon my mind. I felt as if there could never be enough of it. Each characteristic sound was too suggestive to be passed over un-noticed. Beneath and around me, I heard the stir of the hotel; the loud voices of guests, landlord, or bar-keeper; steps echoing on the staircase; the ringing of a bell, an-nouncing arrivals or departures; the porter lumbering past my door with baggage which he thumped down upon the floors of neighboring chambers; the lighter feet of chamber-maids scudding along the passages;—it is ridiculous to think what an interest they had for me! From the street came the

tumult of the pavements, pervading the whole house with
a continual uproar, so broad and deep that only an unaccustomed ear would dwell upon it. A company of the city
soldiery, with a full military band, marched in front of the
hotel, invisible to me, but stirringly audible both by its foot-
tramp and the clangor of its instruments. Once or twice all
the city bells jangled together, announcing a fire, which
brought out the enginemen and their machines, like an army
with its artillery rushing to battle. Hour by hour the clocks
in many steeples responded one to another. In some public
hall, not a great way off, there seemed to be an exhibition
of a mechanical diorama; for, three times during the day,
occurred a repetition of obstreperous music, winding up
with the rattle of imitative cannon and musketry, and a
huge final explosion. Then ensued the applause of the spectators, with clap of hands and thump of sticks, and the
energetic pounding of their heels. All this was just as valu-
able, in its way, as the sighing of the breeze among the
birch-trees that overshadowed Eliot's pulpit. [VIII, 208-210]

With a fairly keen feeling for musical structure and an
accurate sense of harmony and rhythm, Hawthorne has composed this sound-producing imagery. The thumping of the
baggage is repeated by the pounding of the spectators' feet.
The porter's bell is echoed and expanded into the jangle of
the fire-bells and later the city clocks. The marching of sol-
diers and the clapping of spectators' hands carry on the
lighter pattern set up by the chambermaids' feet. The tempo
of the whole is established by the "steps echoing on the staircase" and reinforced at regular intervals by the striking of
the clocks. The entire composition is indirectly broken into
three movements by the "huge final explosion" of the
mechanical diorama. All through this passage, Hawthorne
has pictured the sounds of the city in bright colors. We are
reminded of the comment in the note-books when he enthu-
siastically describes the noises of London and then sums it
all up with the words "that grand lullaby."

6. "The Artist of the Beautiful"

"To the artist, beauty consists of a fine arrangement of line and tone, mass and color."—GEORGE J. COX, *Art*.

———•••———

NOT ALL OF Hawthorne's stories are by any means perfect in respect to form. Many are striking, unified in mood, and intensely emotional—but are still artistically weak. Often they have two or three of the elements of form, but rarely, as in "The Artist of the Beautiful," do they embody almost all the elements. Because it is desirable to keep one of the short stories intact (as we shall do with *The Scarlet Letter* in the next chapter) and because of its rather obvious and satisfactory form, "The Artist of the Beautiful" will be given special consideration. At least from the point of view of this study, the story of Owen Warland and his mechanical butterfly is Hawthorne's most interesting short story, though by no means his best tale.

The over-all structure, the floor-plan, of "The Artist of the Beautiful" is simple and symmetrical. The story, like others we have observed, falls into seven parts. There are four major sections separated by three minor ones. The parts are not equal in length, but nevertheless form a remarkable pattern. Within a few lines, the length of the parts is as follows: *270*, 125, 75, 60, 60, 100, *320*. (The italicized figures indicate the major sections.) The symmetry here is clear when you count the lines, though it is not particularly noticeable when you are reading the story. It is present, nevertheless, and certainly has as much effect on the reader as the subtle composition of a picture has on its observer. Hawthorne makes the last section the longest, but it is intense and fast-moving and its length is not felt. He makes the two middle major sections (the third and fifth) of about the same length. The first major section has to be fairly long to allow space for the necessary exposition, stage-setting, prefiguration, and so on. The three minor sections, which describe periods of inactivity in Owen Warland's life, are roughly symmetrical. The four parts of the story which we have termed major include the action, the progress, of the narrative. In these Owen Warland is working on his butterfly. In the minor sections, he has turned away from the butterfly. The reader, approaching the story for the first or even second time, will feel the ebb and flow of activity, but he may not be aware of the pattern which it follows. I do not mean to imply here, or elsewhere in this study, that pattern is prerequisite to a good story, or that two hundred lines of prose are necessarily *longer* than a hundred and fifty. This would be taking a much too mechanical attitude toward art, an attitude which I should be the first to abhor. Ten lines of Walter Pater, for example, can be as *long* as fifty lines of P. G. Wodehouse. A story with a vague pattern, such as "Drowne's Wooden Image," can be as good a story as "The Artist of the Beautiful." Sheer space and design, however, do contribute to the emotional content of a work of art and do have some effect on the reader or the observer. Furthermore, as it is the purpose of this book to note such details, their presence interests us.

When we look carefully at each of the parts, we find further evidence of the planned structure of this story. It is based on rhythm and repetition. In part one, the principal characters are introduced. A motif which is important to the development of the tale is begun: Peter Hovenden, looking at the watch-maker, says, " 'It would be a flight beyond his usual foolery to seek for the perpetual motion.' " [v, 289] This idea of perpetual motion is a significant theme, as we shall see. Another important motif is first expressed in the early part of the story when Hawthorne describes the might of Robert Danforth, the blacksmith. Danforth's strength is a prefiguration which eventually resolves in the strength of his child. It is in this first part of the story that the butterfly is *suggested* though not specifically mentioned:

> From the time that his little fingers could grasp a pen-knife, Owen had been remarkable for a delicate ingenuity, which sometimes produced pretty shapes in wood, principally figures of flowers and birds, and sometimes seemed to aim at the hidden mysteries of mechanism. But it was always for purposes of grace, and never with any mockery of the useful. . . . he was attempting to imitate the beautiful movements of Nature as exemplified in the flight of birds or the activity of little animals. [v, 292-93]

These phrases, "delicate ingenuity . . . pretty shapes . . . flowers and birds . . . purposes of grace," suggest the butterfly; and "hidden mysteries of mechanism . . . to imitate the beautiful movements of nature" suggest the mechanical. These remarks, along with Owen's whole characterization, pave the way for the mechanical butterfly. When Annie passes outside Owen's shop, his love forces him to discontinue work on his mechanism. Danforth's appearance further upsets him. Danforth comments on the strength of his own mighty arm, which Owen calls " 'an earthly monster.' " The blacksmith says to him: " 'Folks do say that you are trying to discover the perpetual motion.' " [v, 297] Another appearance of these two themes! Owen denies any interest in perpetual motion or in any practical application of mechanics. He does not want " 'the paternity of a new kind of cotton machine.' " [v, 298] Danforth sees no chance of this: " 'No child of yours will have iron joints and sinews,' " he declares. When Owen tries to continue work on the mechanism, he finds that the influence of Danforth has been too great. " 'It has bewildered me, and obscured my perception. I have made the very stroke—the fatal stroke—that I have dreaded from the first!' " [v, 299] The butterfly (although we do not yet know what it is) has been harmed.

Part two, the first of the minor sections, is an interlude in Owen's progress. Discouraged by the destruction of the mechanism, Owen turns to his profession of clock-making and repairing with more interest and vigor than he has ever before shown. Old Peter Hovenden calls on him to commend his work and to urge him to give up his " 'nonsensical trash about the beautiful.' " [v, 301] Hovenden picks up the delicate machine and though he does not harm it further, Owen is frightened. (This act in itself is, of course, a prefiguration.) As a result of this and of Hovenden's "uplifted finger, and a sneer upon his face" Owen begins to let his work decline and starts to wander in the woods and fields. Here he becomes fascinated by the butterflies, as he had been when he was a child:

> Owen Warland felt the impulse to give external reality to his ideas as irresistibly as any of the poets or painters who have arrayed the world in a dimmer and fainter beauty, imperfectly copied from the richness of their visions. [v, 305]

The third part of the story opens with his turning again to creation; and the reader begins to realize that the little mechanism is a butterfly. It is in this third part that Annie comes to his shop and accuses him of having " 'taken up with the notion of putting spirit into machinery.' " [v, 306] This is Annie's version of the idea which Hovenden and Danforth called "perpetual motion." It is not a new theme in the story; it is a modification of an old one. We see this more clearly when Annie picks up the " 'little whirligig, so delicately wrought' " and exclaims, " 'See! I will put it in motion.' " [v, 307] This blended motif will appear later. Annie points at the mechanism with her needle and gives it the "slightest possible touch," but it is enough to ruin it. The first major section of the story concluded with Owen's accidental destruction of the butterfly, and now the second major section ends with Annie's accidental destruction of it.

The fourth section, which is the second minor part, deals

chiefly with Owen's decline. He has given up all pretense of work, both watch-making and butterfly-making. He has begun to drink. Hawthorne does not make much of this, and there is no hint of condemnation. In the midst of one of his drinking parties, Owen sees a butterfly again. The second interlude thus concludes much as the first one did.

Section five shows him turning again to the butterfly. Hawthorne repeats the scheme with which he began section three. Just as Danforth visited him in part one, and Annie in part three, so does Hovenden in part five. And just as both Danforth's and Annie's visit brought harm to the butterfly, so does Hovenden's. Only this time it is the news of Annie's engagement which brings about the destruction, and it is Owen's own hand which causes the damage. Hawthorne repeats the pattern, but with enough variation to avoid monotony—one of the greatest sins in art.

Part six, the third minor part, furthers the degeneration of Owen Warland. He who has dreamed of spiritualizing machinery now abandons his dream. He now prides himself on disclaiming what he had formerly held first in his creed. He makes fun of all attempts to produce beauty and to mechanize it. But, Hawthorne warns us, "in Owen Warland the spirit was not dead nor passed away; it only slept." [v, 316]

> How it awoke again is not recorded. Perhaps the torpid slumber was broken by a convulsive pain. Perhaps, as in a former instance, the butterfly came and hovered about his head and reinspired him—as indeed this creature of the sunshine had always a mysterious mission for the artist,—reinspired him with the former purpose of his life. [v, 316-17]

Hawthorne again avoids monotonous repetition by denying complete knowledge of the matter. But he leaves the reader, who unconsciously looks for symbolic repetition, with the impression that Owen again sees a real butterfly.

The seventh part opens, as the first, third, and fifth did,

with Owen eagerly working on the butterfly: " 'Now for my task,' said he. 'Never did I feel such strength for it as now.' " [v, 317] Hawthorne helps to create suspense by departing from the story and devoting a page to a philosophical discussion of art and death. Then, to help balance the picture, Owen calls on Annie, Danforth, and Hovenden. The child of Annie and Danforth is playing on the floor when he arrives. Owen gives the now completed mechanical butterfly to Annie, as a wedding gift. Her first remark is: " 'Beautiful! Beautiful! . . . Is it alive? Is it alive?' " [v, 322] Thus the motif which began with perpetual motion and continued with the idea of putting spirit into machinery is fully developed in the life which Owen has given to a mechanical butterfly. Annie repeats: " 'But is it alive? . . . Tell me if it be alive, or whether you created it.' " [v, 323-24] And Owen's answer puts the final period to the motif and to the theme of the story: " 'Wherefore ask who created it, so it be beautiful?' " Danforth comments that the butterfly " 'does beat all nature!' " And then he adds, " 'There is more real use in one downright blow of my sledge-hammer . . .' " [v, 325] And so Hawthorne picks up again the thread which was first spun at the beginning of the story, the motif of Danforth's great strength. The butterfly flies gayly around the room:

> . . . but while it still hovered in the air, the little child of strength, with his grandsire's sharp and shrewd expression in his face, made a snatch at the marvelous insect and compressed it in his hand. Annie screamed. Old Peter Hovenden burst into a cold and scornful laugh. The blacksmith, by main force, unclosed the infant's hand, and found within the palm a small heap of glittering fragments, whence the mystery of beauty had fled forever. [v, 329-30]

This, then, completes the motif of Danforth's strength. His son, the "child of strength," the child who does have " 'iron joints and sinews' " wrecks the mechanical butterfly for all time. Owen, of course, is untouched by this disaster: he has created the butterfly and it is beautiful.

So we complete the structural analysis of "The Artist of the Beautiful." The story's pattern is as closely knit and compact as its plot and symbolism. In one sense, I admit, much of what we have been looking at in this analysis might be called symbolism. The butterfly itself is a symbol just as Owen's search for beauty is, or Danforth's strength, or the child. But symbols in literature are a matter of meaning; and in this study we are not interested in meaning. These elements are also a part of the pattern of the story. (They exist independent of the plot or its meaning. We are here justified in viewing them not as elements in the content but as elements in the form. This point of view does not disclaim their importance to the content; it merely ignores it.) Within the seven-part structure, Hawthorne has woven the two principal threads which we have followed. He has given similar but not identical patterns to the several parts, and he has composed the whole on a very neat and tight structural plan. Over this he has laid the story: the content within the form and supported by it.

"The Artist of the Beautiful" does not contain much actual color. There are really only two bright spots, one in part one and the other in part seven. The first is typical of Hawthorne, light and dark with a touch of red. It is a framed picture, too, as seen by Hovenden and his daughter through the door of the blacksmith shop:

> Within was seen the forge, now blazing up and illuminating the high and dusky roof, and now confining its lustre to a narrow precinct of the coal-strewn floor, according as the breath of the bellows was puffed forth or again inhaled into its vast leathern lungs. In the intervals of brightness it was easy to distinguish objects in remote corners of the shop and the horseshoes that hung upon the wall; in the momentary gloom, the fire seemed to be glimmering amidst the vagueness of unenclosed space. Moving about in this red glare and alternate dusk was the figure of the blacksmith, well worthy to be viewed in so picturesque an aspect of light and shade, where the bright blaze struggled with the black night,

as if each would have snatched his comely strength from the other. Anon he drew a white-hot bar of iron from the coals, laid it on the anvil, uplifted his arm of might, and was seen enveloped in the myriads of sparks which the strokes of the hammer scattered into the surrounding gloom. [v, 290-91]

One glaring spot of red in the centre of a fluctuating black and white field! The "myriads of sparks" is repeated at the end of the tale in Owen's butterfly:

The rich down was visible upon its wings; the lustre of its eyes seemed instinct with spirit. The firelight glimmered around this wonder—the candles gleamed upon it; but it glistened apparently by its own radiance, and illuminated the finger and outstretched hand on which it rested with a white gleam like that of precious stones. [v, 322]

Annie later places the butterfly on her father's finger:

Even the bright spots of gold upon its wings and body, unless her eyes deceived her, grew dim, and the glowing purple took a dusky hue, and the starry lustre that gleamed around the blacksmith's hand became faint, and vanished. [v, 327]

Then Danforth takes the insect again:

. . . its hues assumed much of their original lustre, and the gleam of starlight, which was its most ethereal attribute, again formed a halo round about it. At first, when transferred from Robert Danforth's hand to the small finger of the child, this radiance grew so powerful that it positively threw the little fellow's shadow back against the wall. [v, 328]

The colorful gleam of the butterfly fluctuates just as the blacksmith's fire does. Hawthorne compares and contrasts the glow from the blacksmith's work with that from Owen's. These two colorful passages are connected, throughout the story, by several areas illuminated by Owen's work-lamp. At one point, he places the delicate mechanism in "the condensed light of his lamp." At another time "his lamp flickered in the socket and left the artist of the Beautiful in darkness." Then, "the gleam of lamplight through the crevices of Owen Warland's shutters" is seen; or "the lines of lamplight through the crevices"; or "the lustre of his lamp on the delicate piece of work." These are unusually fine examples of Hawthorne's use of spot-lights as well as of his unification of details by rhythmic repetition.

There is some color, too, or at least black and white, in the jewel-box which housed the butterfly. But of more interest than color is the movement:

> It was carved richly out of ebony by his own hand, and inlaid with a fanciful tracery of pearl, representing a boy in pursuit of a butterfly, which, elsewhere, had become a winged spirit, and was flying heavenward; while the boy, or youth, had found such efficacy in his strong desire that he ascended from earth to cloud, and from cloud to celestial atmosphere, to win the beautiful. [v, 321-22]

Probably the box was decorated with a kind of frieze in which different stages in an action are pictured simultaneously. Whatever the method of Owen's picture, Hawthorne's picture has an upward movement which is most effective. There is movement, too, in the flight of the mechanical insect. Three short passages will picture it for us:

> The butterfly now flung itself upon the air, fluttered round Annie's head, and soared into a distant region of the parlor, still making itself perceptible to sight by the starry gleam in which the motion of its wings enveloped it. The infant on the floor followed its course with his sagacious little eyes. After flying about the room, it returned in a spiral curve and settled again on Annie's finger. [v, 323]

Hawthorne wisely uses the words "distant region" to give length to the soaring curve of the butterfly's flight, and the movement of the child's eye helps the reader empathically to visualize the line. The "spiral curve" is particularly graphic. The author's phrase "settled again on Annie's finger" helps to define the line by terminating it. Here again, words on the page, which have no intrinsic aesthetic content, produce mental images which have strong aesthetic content. Two more flights are made by the butterfly before it dies.

> . . . then, ascending from the blacksmith's stalwart finger,
> it rose in a gradually enlarging curve to the ceiling, made
> one wide sweep around the room, and returned with an
> undulating movement to the point whence it had started.
> [v, 324-25]

And finally we see the same wide-sweeping circle that moves
in space as the butterfly makes its last flight:

> At length it arose from the small hand of the infant with
> an airy motion that seemed to bear it upward without an ef-
> fort, as if the ethereal instincts with which its master's spirit
> had endowed it impelled this fair vision involuntarily to a
> higher sphere. Had there been no obstruction, it might have
> soared into the sky and grown immortal. But its lustre
> gleamed upon the ceiling; the exquisite texture of its wings
> brushed against that earthly medium; and a sparkle or two,
> as of star-dust, floated downward and lay glimmering on the
> carpet. Then the butterfly came fluttering down, and, in-
> stead of returning to the infant, was apparently attracted to-
> wards the artist's hand. [v, 328-29]

Here the upward line is even longer and higher, and by way
of contrast the author draws in some fluttering, downward
lines of "star dust," another repetition of the blacksmith's
forge. All three of these passages suggest the diagonal, curv-
ing movement of lines. And by the expansion of these lines
into space, mass is indicated: we are able to visualize something of the room's size in three dimensions.

Hawthorne achieves a kind of crescendo through rhythm
in this story. I have called rhythm the more-or-less regular
repetition of a motif. With more-or-less regularity Hawthorne repeats the words *butterfly* and *beautiful* (or some
form of them). It will be worth while to look at a list of
these repeated motifs.

Section   I: beautiful, Beautiful, beautiful, Beauty, beautiful,
              Beautiful.
         II: Beautiful, butterfly, butterflies, butterflies, butter-
              fly, butterflies, Beautiful.

III: beauty.

IV: butterfly.

V: butterfly, butterfly, Beautiful, Beautiful, Beautiful.

VI: butterfly.

VII: beauty, Beautiful, Beautiful, Beautiful, Beautiful, Beauty, butterfly, Beautiful, butterfly, butterfly, beauty, Beautiful, Beautiful, butterfly, butterfly, butterfly, beautiful, butterfly, beauty, butterfly, butterfly, butterfly, Beautiful, Beautiful, butterfly, butterfly, butterfly, butterfly, butterfly, butterfly, butterfly, butterfly, butterfly, Beautiful.

After a little counting, we find that there is an average of about two of these words to the page, a frequency which demands attention. The pattern is established in the first two sections of the story; the frequency is reduced in the middle parts; and it increases in a definite crescendo in the last part. This is a small matter and one which might be considered accidental and unimportant; but I have no doubt that the repetition of these words has an artistic and emotional effect in prose just as it would have in poetry.

The structure of the story and the motifs in it are undoubtedly worked out according to a pattern. To say that there is anything like dynamic symmetry may be stretching the point too far. But there is symmetry and it is dynamic in so far as it is intrinsic in the very life of the tale and is interwoven with the content and its symbolism. The whole thing is too compact and symmetrical to be accidental. The mind and emotions of an artist are so intricate that we cannot safely claim that this patterned form is the result either of conscious or of unconscious activity. We can only say that the story is certainly well planned, that the plan was designed intentionally, and that perhaps it was designed consciously.

7. The Scarlet Letter

". . . 'The Scarlet Letter' is a perfect book. No word, no suggestion, no detail or scene, but is set in its place with sure artistry. Hawthorne knew thoroughly the nature and methods of his art. He did not stumble into success, but worked with his eyes open."—JOHN MACY, *The Spirit of American Literature.*

———•••———

The Scarlet Letter, as John Macy says, is a perfect book. Henry A. Beers points out that it is Hawthorne's "most intensely conceived work, the most thoroughly fused and logically developed."[1] Henry James says that it is "more complete" than Hawthorne's other novels, that "it achieves more perfectly what it attempts, and it has about it that charm . . . which we find in an artist's work the first time he has touched his highest mark."[2] A dozen other critics could be cited to support the claim that it is not only Hawthorne's finest work of art but also one of the great art products of all literature. Certainly such a book as this deserves a chapter to itself.[3]

It is unfortunate that this study has had to dissect so many of Hawthorne's works and to separate parts from their wholes. To avoid repetition as well as to point out and stress

---

[1] *Four Americans* (New Haven, Yale University Press, 1920), p. 46.

[2] *Hawthorne* (New York, Harper and Brothers, 1879), p. 107.

[3] One comment, typical of many, is this of Carl H. Grabo: "The charm of the book lies greatly in its mystery, in its massing of light and shade; in its occasional high lights, but more in its dim shadows suggesting so much but explicitly outlining so little. It reminds one of the masterpieces of Rembrandt, low-keyed, wonderfully massed, with a sure emphasis upon the face or figure which could command and hold the eye, and grouped around this focal point other figures less emphatic and subtly graduated. The art is highly selective. Out of the many figures only a few are identified; and yet the background is solid and populous. The aesthetic sense is gratified; these calculated and yet seemingly simple effects are art."—*The Technique of the Novel* (New York, Charles Scribner's Sons, 1928), p. 52.

certain design elements, this procedure has seemed desirable. But here, *The Scarlet Letter,* we must hold the book together.

In one sense all that comes before this chapter is introductory to it. Our consideration of pattern, rhythm, balance, and the other elements of form, as well as the brief analysis of "The Artist of the Beautiful," should help to make the beauty of form in *The Scarlet Letter* more apparent. Not that form in this book is so subtle. It is not. Lewis E. Gates notices its obvious artificiality: the overt use of symbols, the throbbing heat of the scarlet letter, the great red "A" in the sky, the shadow on Dimmesdale.[4] Of course these things are artificial—at least they are not untouched nature displayed without selection. But, as we have said before, all art is necessarily artificial. When art is nature, it is no longer art. Hawthorne has selected, arranged, and emphasized his material to produce a work of art according to a preconceived plan. We shall be able to see this plan the better for having observed the author's methods in other works.

The structural plan of *The Scarlet Letter* is one of its most beautiful and artistic qualities. No really great work of art is absolutely geometric in its composition. Even the "Last Supper" of Leonardo—so neat in its mathematics—is not flawless in this respect. The good artist avoids absolute balance, absolute repetition, absolute rhythm. Hawthorne has come as close to the absolute in *The Scarlet Letter* as he safely could. The novel's introduction, "The Custom House," is at once a part of the story and separate from it. It is joined to the story by its reference to the letter and by its title which sounds and looks like the titles of the chapters in the novel. (This is the only instance in which the introduction to a Hawthorne novel has a specific and descriptive title.) "The Custom House" is separate from the story in that it is not a first chapter; it is frankly introductory. The last chapter of the book is called "Conclusion." It has a chapter number, twenty-four, and is thus structurally tied into the story. But

---

[4] *Studies and Appreciations* (New York, Macmillan Co., 1900), p. 105.

it, too, is separate from the main flow. It is a summary which ties the various threads together; and it leaps ahead in time, it explains what becomes of the characters. It is related to "The Custom House" by a reference to the "manuscript of old date," described in the introduction, and by a mention of Mr. Surveyor Pue who figures in "The Custom House." Thus the introduction and the conclusion constitute a kind of frame around the story of Hester Prynne. It is true that this frame is not built in quite the same way as many of Hawthorne's frames are, and that it is not perfectly balanced. But its two sections are as much separated from the main story as they are related to it; and I think we may treat them either as a structural part of the story or as a frame. For the sake of simplifying the analysis of the novel's structure, I have chosen to think of "The Custom House" and "Conclusion" as a frame, apart from the story itself.

When we make this separation, the pattern of the story becomes clear and beautiful. It is built around the scaffold. At the beginning, in the middle, and at the end of the story the scaffold is the dominating point. Just as it literally rises above the market-place, so does it structurally rise out of the novel's plan and attribute pattern to it. In chapter two, after the very short first chapter, Hester is taken up on the scaffold. In chapter twelve, the middle chapter (when we omit the concluding chapter), Dimmesdale mounts the scaffold. In chapter twenty-three, the last (omitting the conclusion), Dimmesdale takes Hester and Pearl up there with him. These three incidents are, in every sense, the high points of the novel. The middle chapter, number twelve, tends to divide the story into two parts (or three parts, counting this middle chapter). This division is logical when we realize that up to chapter twelve neither the reader nor Chillingworth is certain that Dimmesdale is the father of little Pearl; after chapter twelve, there can be no doubt.

There is more to the pattern than this two-fold division. The scaffold, in Boston, stands in the market-place. The setting of the first three and the last three chapters is the market-place. In the first three chapters, Hester's ignominy is established. The last three chapters build up to and include Dimmesdale's victory over Chillingworth. Thus these two groups of chapters are set-off from the remainder of the story by locale as well as by function. The chapters between the first three and the middle one fall nicely into two groups of five and three chapters each. The group of five—chapters four through eight—deal chiefly with Pearl and Hester and describe Hester's struggles in the community. The group of three—chapters nine, ten, and eleven—deal with Chillingworth and Dimmesdale and show Chillingworth gaining the minister's confidence and digging out his secret. There are also eight chapters between chapter twelve and the last three, and they, too, fall into two groups of three and five chapters each. The group of three—chapters thirteen, fourteen, and fifteen—deal with Hester and Pearl again and indicate Hester's improved condition both in the community and within herself. The group of five—chapters sixteen through twenty—show the partial reunion of Hester and Dimmesdale and their growing resistance to Chillingworth's power.

So it is that we find *The Scarlet Letter* falling into a structural pattern of seven parts (exclusive of the frame), as many of Hawthorne's stories tend to do. As we shall see, when we consider color in the novel, the color distribution supports this seven-part division. For the sake of clarity, we can indicate this division graphically. (See chart on next page.)

We may, if we wish, think of this novel as a drama, a tragedy. Henry A. Beers says that the great difference between *The House of the Seven Gables* and *The Scarlet Letter* is the difference between romance and tragedy.[5] (In this connection it is interesting to read in the note-books that *The Scarlet Letter*, in Hawthorne's opinion, might make a good opera but would never make a good play.) [XIX, 378] If we

---

[5] *Four Americans*, p. 46.

"The Custom-House"			*Framework*
	I	"The Prison-door"	
A	II	"The Market-place"	*Hester on the scaffold*
	III	"The Recognition"	
	IV	"The Interview"	
	V	"Hester at her Needle"	
B	VI	"Pearl"	*Hester and Pearl strug-*
	VII	"The Governor's Hall"	*gling*
	VIII	"The Elf-child and the Minister"	
	IX	"The Leech"	
C	X	"The Leech and his Patient"	*Chillingworth's progress*
	XI	"The Interior of a Heart"	
D	XII	"The Minister's Vigil"	*Dimmesdale on the scaffold*
	XIII	"Another View of Hester"	
E	XIV	"Hester and the Physician"	*Hester and Pearl rising*
	XV	"Hester and Pearl"	
	XVI	"A Forest Walk"	
	XVII	"The Pastor and his Parishioner"	*Hester and Dimmesdale*
F	XVIII	"A Flood of Sunshine"	*rise as Chillingworth*
	XIX	"The Child at the Brook-side"	*falls*
	XX	"The Minister in a Maze"	
	XXI	"The New England Holiday"	*Hester, Pearl and*
G	XXII	"The Procession"	*Dimmesdale on the*
	XXIII	"The Revelation of the Scarlet Letter"	*scaffold*
	XXIV	"Conclusion"	*Framework*

divide the novel into three parts of eight chapters each, we can see a pattern which might lend itself to dramatic form. However, this novel, like all good novels, is not really suited to play form. It is too large in its sweep, too gentle in its movement, too leisurely in its progress. It is not, as George Pierce Baker often defined a play, the shortest line from emotion to emotion. In two parts or in three parts or better yet in seven parts, it is a beautifully constructed novel.

Like "The Minister's Black Veil" and "Rappaccini's Daughter," *The Scarlet Letter* has vibrancy of movement. The scarlet of Hester's token vibrates in its brilliancy. Sunlight and shadow flicker in and out of the picture. Pearl's constant motion keeps the eye moving. There are, in addition, many little images of trembling motion. In chapter four, which describes the interview between Hester and Chillingworth, the three-month-old baby is pictured as being violently upset. "It now writhed in convulsions of pain" and "she lay writhing on the trundlebed," and after the physician had given her some medicine, "its convulsive tossings gradually ceased." Seven years later, when Hester is trying to make Pearl and Dimmesdale become friends, Pearl "now suddenly burst into a fit of passion, gesticulating violently and throwing her small figure in the most extravagant contortions." [vi, 303] Dimmesdale's voice, when he is talking to Chillingworth, is "more tremulous than before," and later he clears his throat and speaks with a "tremulous breath." When Chillingworth opens the minister's shirt to examine him, "Mr. Dimmesdale shuddered, and slightly stirred." [vi, 197] On the scaffold, in the middle chapter, the minister sees the physician in the darkness and says, " 'I shiver at him! . . . I tell thee, my soul shivers at him!' " And when, in chapter twenty-three, he is determined to reveal his own scarlet letter, he tears off his ministerial garb "with a convulsive motion." When Hester is thinking of Dimmesdale, her soul is moved "by the shuddering terror with which he had appealed to her." Even nature helps to convey this trembling movement to the story. "The forest . . . creaked with a blast that was passing through it. The boughs were tossing heavily above their heads." The sunlight conveniently flickers to keep Dimmesdale in the shadow; and the sky, on the night of the minister's vigil, trembles with strange lights. Hawthorne has enlivened the story by these bits of vibrating motion.

Of the many rhythmic motifs in *The Scarlet Letter* none is so powerful or so simple as the scarlet letter itself. Functionally, I suppose, the letter is a moral symbol, but artistically it is a glorious red spot, which, as John Macy says, "appealed less to [Hawthorne's] moral sense than to his pictorial imagination."[6] And how cleverly Hawthorne handles it! He never tells us in so many words what the "A" stands for; but there is no doubt in our minds. It is referred to first in chapter two as "the mark," "a certain token," and finally as "the letter A." Then it is called, in capital letters, "the SCARLET LETTER." Then it is "the red letter," "the scarlet letter," "the ignominious letter," "the letter A," and again "the scarlet letter." Nine times in the first chapter in which it appears, chapter two, it is mentioned. Nearly a hundred and fifty times throughout the book does Hawthorne, in one way or another, refer to this symbol. Sixty percent of the times he calls it by its full name, "the scarlet letter." At other times it is "the embroidered letter," or "the ignominious brand," or "the fatal symbol," or any one of a number of other names. It appears on the average of more than once every two pages. We are never allowed to forget it. Its greatest frequency is in part B, the five chapters which deal with the struggles of Pearl and Hester, where it appears forty times. Then, with his fine sense of contrast, Hawthorne uses it only twice in the next three chapters, part C. In the middle chapter it is used three times: once it is "the embroidered letter glowing upon her bosom," and the other two times it is the "letter A" glowing in the sky. Interestingly, the frequency of its use is divided almost equally between the first and second halves of the novel. Then, just by way of topping it all, in his "Conclusion," Hawthorne describes Dimmesdale and Hester as both buried under the same tombstone on which is inscribed: "On a Field, sable, the letter A, gules." There are only three chapters in which the scarlet letter does not appear: chapter one, the short first

---

[6] Mr. Macy goes on to say: "He turned the symbol over and over, and embroidered his story with it. It is a red spot on a gray colonial dress. It is a bloody brand on a man's breast. It is a fiery portent in the sky. Hawthorne was enamoured of its hue and he designed it cunningly like a worker in tapestry against the tortured conscience of Dimmesdale, and against Chillingworth, the skulking ghost of revenge."—*The Spirit of American Literature* (Garden City, Doubleday, Page and Co., 1913), p. 84.

chapter; chapter nine, dealing entirely with Chillingworth; and chapter twenty, dealing entirely with Dimmesdale. Hawthorne uses his symbol with great care, putting it where it is most needed, and making it possibly the most dominating symbol in all literature.

After the scarlet letter, other motifs in the novel are sure to seem pale. But there are several others well worth considering. Related to the motif of Hester's brand is that of Dimmesdale's. We first read of the minister's often repeated gesture in chapter three, when he is urging Hester to reveal the child's father. He is described as speaking to her and "leaning over the balcony, with his hand upon his heart." In the next chapter, when Chillingworth is also urging her to tell the man's name, he speaks of this unknown villain and says, " 'He bears no letter of infamy wrought into his garments, as thou dost; but I shall read it in his heart.' " When we next see Dimmesdale, in chapter eight, Hester and Pearl are at the Governor's house. Hester turns to the minister for support in her request that she be allowed to keep Pearl:

> . . . the young minister at once came forward, pale, and holding his hand over his heart, as was his custom whenever his peculiarly nervous temperament was thrown into agitation. He looked now more careworn and emaciated than as we described him at the scene of Hester's public ignominy; and whether it were his failing health, or whatever the cause might be, his large dark eyes had a world of pain in their troubled and melancholy depth. [VI, 161]

The reader does not know, at this point, although he may suspect it, that Dimmesdale is Pearl's father. The minister's gesture of putting his hand over his heart may be an habitual one started many years before. But there is little doubt that Hawthorne intends the gesture to be related to Dimmesdale's own private scarlet letter which has evidently been growing increasingly vivid and painful. In chapter nine, Hawthorne describes this action three times. In the next chapter, ten, the minister and Chillingworth are talking about Hester, and Dimmesdale says, "it must needs be better for the sufferer to be free to show his pain, as this poor woman Hester is, than to cover it all up in his heart." [VI, 192] It is only a few pages later, while Dimmesdale is sleeping, that Chillingworth makes his discovery:

> The physician advanced directly in front of his patient, laid his hand upon his bosom, and thrust aside the vestment that, hitherto, had always covered it even from the professional eye.
>
> Then, indeed, Mr. Dimmesdale shuddered, and slightly stirred.
>
> After a brief pause, the physician turned away.
>
> But with what a wild look of wonder, joy, and horror! [VI, 197]

In the next chapter, Hawthorne speaks of Chillingworth as a diabolic magician who can call up "many shapes, of death, or more awful shame, all flocking around about the clergy-man, and pointing with their fingers at his breast!" And later in the same chapter Dimmesdale imagines that Hester has led Pearl into his study. He thinks he sees Pearl "in her scarlet garb, and pointing her forefinger, first at the scarlet letter on her bosom, and then at the clergyman's own breast." The following chapter tells of the minister's vigil on the scaffold at night:

> . . . Mr. Dimmesdale was overcome with a great horror of mind, as if the universe were gazing at a scarlet token on his naked breast, right over his heart. On that spot, in very truth, there was, and there had long been, the gnawing and poisonous tooth of bodily pain. [VI, 212]

Later Pearl and Hester join the minister on the scaffold and Hawthorne writes:

> And there stood the minister, with his hand over his heart; and Hester Prynne, with the embroidered letter glimmering on her bosom; and little Pearl, herself a symbol, and the connecting link between these two. [VI, 220-21]

The phrase "herself a symbol" seems to connect the minister's gesture with the symbol on his own heart. In chapter fifteen,

Pearl asks three times why the minister keeps his hand over his heart; and twice in the following chapter she comments on this strange gesture. In chapter seventeen, when Hester is trying to give courage and strength to Dimmesdale, he tells her that she can be happy because she wears her scarlet letter openly while " 'Mine burns in secret!' " And then, when she tells him that Chillingworth is really his enemy, he starts to his feet, "gasping for breath, and clutching at his heart, as if he would have torn it out of his bosom." [vi, 278] Once more in the same chapter he cries out, "pressing his hand nervously against his heart,—a gesture that had grown involuntary with him." A few pages later, in the next chapter, he repeats the gesture and Pearl again asks about it. In chapter twenty, we see Dimmesdale "white and speechless, with one hand on the Hebrew Scriptures, and the other spread upon his breast." Pearl again comments on the minister's gesture, in chapters twenty-one and twenty-two. Even the old witch, Mistress Hibbins, mentions it twice. At the end of chapter twenty-two, Hawthorne writes:

> The sainted minister in the church! The woman of the scarlet letter in the market-place! What imagination would have been irreverent enough to surmise that the same scorching stigma was on them both! [vi, 358]

In chapter twenty-three, he mounts the scaffold and says to his people, " 'But there stood one in the midst of you, at whose brand of sin and infamy ye have not shuddered!' "

> "Now, at the death-hour, he stands up before you! He bids you look again at Hester's scarlet letter! He tells you that, with all its mysterious horror, it is but the shadow of what he bears on his own breast, and that even this, his own red stigma, is no more than the type of what has seared his inmost heart! Stand any here that question God's judgment on a sinner? Behold! Behold a dreadful witness of it!"
> [vi, 370]

As Dimmesdale dies, he exclaims that God has shown him mercy by giving him "this burning torture" to bear upon his breast. In the "Conclusion," Hawthorne notes that some who were present at Dimmesdale's confession "testified to having seen, on the breast of the unhappy minister, a SCARLET LETTER." This concludes the rhythmic motif.

It is a long motif, extending from nearly the beginning of the story to its end, and appearing on thirty different pages of the book. I have taken the time and space necessary to trace it through the novel because it is one of the finest and most varied examples of a rhythmic motif in Hawthorne. It is more, even, than a good prefiguration; it is a whole story in itself. We have seen how the author can spin into a single thread many elements: Dimmesdale's guilt, his habitual gesture, the gnawing pain, his gradual weakness and decline, and even Pearl's increasing alertness. It fills out the meaning of the scarlet letter while it is pointing to the climax of the story. It follows the pattern of the novel by beginning with Hester's appearance on the scaffold, achieving a supernatural quality on the scaffold in the twelfth chapter, and culminating with the revelation on the scaffold at the end of the book. This motif has the weakness of any often repeated device: it becomes monotonous. But it must be remembered that this is not as apparent when it is spread out through the novel as it has been in the condensed version of our analysis.

Another prefiguration which leads up to the scene in the last chapter is one dealing with Hester, Pearl, and Dimmesdale. It is a much shorter sequence than the one we have just followed, but it is equally important to the story and equally impressive. It begins, rather indirectly, in chapter five:

> There dwelt, there trode the feet of one with whom she deemed herself connected in a union, that, unrecognized on earth, would bring them together before the bar of final judgment, and make that their marriage altar, for a joint futurity of endless retribution. [VI, 113]

This is just a suggestion, a vague hint. In the light of what follows, it appears to be the introduction to a prefiguration.

It is not until the middle chapter of the book that the motif really gets a good start. Pearl and Hester have joined Dimmesdale on the scaffold, and Pearl asks, " 'Wilt thou stand here with mother and me, to-morrow noontide?' " [vi, 219] Dimmesdale cannot agree to do this, but he does promise to take their hands at a later time: " 'before the judgment-seat, thy mother and thou and I must stand to-gether.' " [vi, 220] Near the end of this chapter Pearl taunts the minister: " 'Thou wouldst not promise to take my hand, and mother's hand, to-morrow noontide.' " Hawthorne leaps over six chapters before he repeats the motif again. In chapter nineteen Pearl wonders whether the three of them can go into town, hand-in-hand. In chapter twenty-three she speaks of it again:

> "What a strange, sad man is he!" said the child, as if speaking partly to herself. "In the dark night-time he calls us to him, and holds thy hand and mine, as when we stood with him on the scaffold yonder. And in the deep forest, where only the old trees can hear and the strip of sky see it, he talks with thee, sitting on a heap of moss! And he kisses my forehead, too, so that the little brook would hardly wash it off! But here, in the sunny day and among all the people, he knows us not; nor must we know him! A strange, sad man is he, with his hand always over his heart!" [vi, 332-33]

Thus, in a paragraph probably planned for the purpose of characterization, Hawthorne connects two' motifs. In the last chapter, as we know, Dimmesdale does join hands with Pearl and Hester on the scaffold, in the light of day and before all his people.

Glimpses of Mistress Hibbins, the witch, are seen several times throughout *The Scarlet Letter*. She is first mentioned at the beginning of the story when Hawthorne notes that the crowd in the market-place, awaiting Hester's appear-ance, is as excited as it would be if Mistress Hibbins were to die upon the gallows. We finally see her at the Governor's house. The old woman, who a few years later "was to be executed as a witch," thrusts her head out of a window and invites Hester to join her at night in the merry company of the Black Man. During Dimmesdale's vigil on the scaffold (chapter twelve), she again thrusts her head from a window, "and looked anxiously upward." When she sees a light in the market-place, she vanishes: "Possibly she went up among the clouds." Pearl mentions her once, and seems to be quite interested in the old woman. Dimmesdale speaks of her. Her wrath, he says, is the only thing which is more upsetting to him than the violent rage of Pearl. While Hester and Pearl are watching the election-procession, Mistress Hibbins joins them and again invites them to come to the forest at night. She implies that Hester is already close to the heart of the Black Man. The old witch knows, or at least guesses, the truth about Hester, Pearl, and Dimmesdale.

Witchcraft cannot be overemphasized in any study of *The Scarlet Letter*. It appears not only in Mistress Hibbins, but also in many small ways through the novel. Both Dimmesdale and Chillingworth are thought to be possessed of the Black Man no less than Hester. Pearl, too, as we learn at many points, is possibly related to the "Prince of the Air." Mistress Hibbins says that he is the little girl's father. There are a number of references to the elf-like quality of Pearl, and frequently it is suggested that there is more of evil in her than of good. She is called "an airy sprite" who "would flit away with a mocking smile." In the same chapter, six, she is "a little imp, whose next freak might be to fly up the chimney." Her mother calls her an "elfish child" and wonders where she came from. The neighbors, "seeking vainly elsewhere for the child's paternity," conclude that "little Pearl was a demon offspring." Old Mr. Wilson, seeing her at the governor's house, wonders whether she is one of those "naughty elfs or fairies, whom we thought to have left behind us," in England. Dimmesdale, after questioning her on her catechism, says, " 'The little baggage hath witchcraft in her, I profess. . . . She needs an old woman's broomstick to fly withal.'" In chapter ten even Chillingworth comments on this quality in the child: "'What, in Heaven's name, is she? Is the imp altogether evil?'" In chapter twelve, Hawthorne says that there "was witchcraft in little Pearl's eyes," and that on her face was "that naughty smile which made its expression frequently so elfish." Hester speaks of her in chapter nineteen as "'a fitful and fantastic little elf, sometimes.'" In his "Conclusion," Hawthorne calls her "the elf-child,—the demon offspring, as some people, up to that epoch, persisted in considering her." These are but a few of the many references in the book to Pearl's elfish nature and her possible connection with witchcraft, but they are sufficient to indicate the manner in which this motif is developed.

One other motif in the novel should be noted. The careful reader of Hawthorne cannot help being aware of the author's acute consciousness of the horror of loneliness. This is perhaps more apparent in *The Scarlet Letter* than in his other works, and it constitutes a sombre motif in the story. In chapter two, Hawthorne tells us that Hester's scarlet emblem "had the effect of a spell, taking her out of the ordinary relations with humanity, and enclosing her in a sphere by herself." When Dimmesdale first appears, chapter three, we learn that he looks like "a being who felt himself quite astray and at a loss in the pathway of human existence, and could only be at ease in some seclusion of his own." Hester's little house, set apart from the town, is described as a "lonesome dwelling." One of the finest summaries of this feeling of loneliness is in chapter five, "Hester at her Needle":

> In all her intercourse with society, however, there was nothing that made her feel as if she belonged to it. Every gesture, every word, and even the silence of those with whom she came in contact, implied, and often expressed, that she was banished, and as much alone as if she inhabited another sphere, or communicated with the common nature by other organs and senses than the rest of human kind. She stood apart from moral interests, yet close beside them, like a ghost that revisits the familiar fireside, and can no longer

make itself seen or felt; no more smile with the household
joy, nor mourn with the kindred sorrow; or, should it
succeed in manifesting its forbidden sympathy, awakening
only terror and horrible repugnance. These emotions, in
fact, and its bitterest scorn besides, seemed to be the sole
portion that she retained in the universal heart. [VI, 119]

She is pictured as "gliding silently through the town, with
never any companion but one only child." Hester refused to
give up her daughter because she was alone in the world,
"cast off by it, with this soul treasure to keep her heart alive."
Pearl, too, is "a born outcast of the infantile world." When
Dimmesdale learns of Chillingworth's villainy, he says,
" 'There is not the strength or courage left me to venture
into the wide, strange, difficult world, alone'."

> He repeated the word.
> "Alone, Hester!"
> "Thou shalt not go alone!" answered she, in a deep whisper.
> Then, all was spoken! [VI, 287]

It is only Chillingworth's loneliness that is not described,
but it is certainly felt.

Before turning away from rhythmic motifs, something
should be said regarding Dimmesdale's guilt and Chillingworth's vengeance. Dimmesdale's connection with Hester's
disgrace is never, in so many words, stated. It gradually
becomes apparent to the reader, just as it does to Chillingworth. Because it is never specifically stated, it can hardly
be said to be prefigured, and yet the hints which Hawthorne
drops along the way form themselves into a rhythmic motif.
We shall simply glance at a few of the high spots in the
development of this sequence. There are a number of hints
in chapters two and three where the townspeople notice
Dimmesdale's deep concern for Hester and her problem. He
is upset that " 'such a scandal should have come upon his
congregation,' " says one of the people. This is only natural,
of course, but the statement has meaning coming as it does

so early in the story. Hester's crime is again linked with the minister when another citizen says, " 'She has raised a great scandal, I promise you, in godly Master Dimmesdale's church.' " In neither of these instances did Hawthorne have to mention Dimmesdale by name. There are other guarded but pointed hints throughout these chapters. In chapter eight, Hester says to Dimmesdale, " 'Thou wast my pastor, and hadst charge of my soul, and knowest me better than these men can.' " Two pages farther on, Dimmesdale states, " 'Herein is the sinful mother happier than the sinful father.' " And on the next page we read that Pearl went up to Dimmesdale "and taking his hand in the grasp of both her own, laid her cheek against it"; a caress "so tender" and "unobtrusive" that even Hester was surprised by it. Chapters nine, ten, and eleven are full of such hints. They range from the generalities of frequent and numerous references to Dimmesdale's declining health to the specific suggestion implied in Dimmesdale's vision of Pearl pointing her finger first at Hester's scarlet letter and then "at the clergyman's own breast." By the middle chapter of the book, it is fairly clear to the reader that Dimmesdale is Pearl's father. When the great scarlet letter glows in the sky, we, and Chillingworth who has been looking on, are convinced. It has all been done subtly. There has been nothing of the suggestiveness or of the evasiveness that a more modern technique might have employed.

The motif of Chillingworth's vengeance follows that of Dimmesdale's guilt, in fact, parallels it, although the revenge motif continues on to the end of the book. We see it first in Chillingworth's interview with Hester in chapter four, when he admits a " 'scheme of vengeance.' " He says that even though the guilty man wear no symbol on his clothes, " 'I shall read it on his heart.' " He promises that he will do nothing to ruin Hester's soul: " 'No, not thine!' " We get the first suggestion of his suspicion when, after the minister has staunchly defended Hester's right to keep her child,

Chillingworth says to him, " 'You speak, my friend, with a strange earnestness.' " [vi, 163] Chapters nine, ten, and eleven deal almost entirely with Dimmesdale's guilt, his decline in health, and the physician's diabolic boring into his confidence. He prods the minister with hypothetical discussions of guilt; he watches him tremble under penetrating glances; he observes, and encourages, his increasing nervous and physical weakness; he constantly haunts Dimmesdale's waking and sleeping hours, and torments him with numerous gentle but piercing stabs. Hester sums it up when she says, " 'You burrow and rankle in his heart! Your clutch is on his life, and you cause him to die daily a living death; and still he knows you not.' " [vi, 245] Chillingworth admits this charge and says, " 'Never did mortal suffer what this man has suffered.' " When Dimmesdale learns the true character of Chillingworth, he claims that the " 'old man's revenge' " is blacker than his own sin. Chillingworth's whole relation to the story and to the characters in it is expressed in terms of vengeance. As the minister, in the last chapter, invites Hester and Pearl to go up on the scaffold with him, Chillingworth makes a final grasp for his victim:

> "Madman, hold! what is your purpose?" whispered he. "Wave back that woman! Cast off this child! All shall be well! Do not blacken your fame, and perish in dishonor! I can yet save you! Would you bring infamy on your sacred profession?" [vi, 366]

But Dimmesdale exclaims that it is too late. He will escape. When the three mount the scaffold, Chillingworth quite frankly admits that " 'there was no one place so secret,—no high place nor lowly place, where thou couldst have escaped me,—save on this very scaffold!' " If the minister's death is what Chillingworth wants, then his vengeance is complete. But we are led to believe that through confession Dimmesdale actually deprives the old physician of the sweetness of revenge. In any case, whatever the moral significance, the revenge motif is strong. It runs throughout the entire book.

With several others we have noted, it helps to unify the novel and to lend rhythm to its form.

By rhythmic repetition, Hawthorne builds up a number of artistic motifs; and by repetition, too, he succeeds in creating several passages of almost poetic charm. The intensity of chapters three and four is supported by four different sets of repeated words and phrases. Chillingworth, speaking of Hester's unknown partner, exclaims: " 'But he will be known!—he will be known!—he will be known!' " [vi, 88] Again, in his interview with Hester, he speaks with poetic fervor:

> "Live, therefore, and bear about thy doom with thee, in the eyes of men and women,—in the eyes of him whom thou didst call thy husband,—in the eyes of yonder child!" [vi, 103-104]

He repeats Hester's statement regarding the identity of the man, " 'That thou shalt never know!' " " 'Never, sayest thou?' rejoined he, with a smile of dark and self-relying intelligence. 'Never know him!' " [vi, 106] And on the next page, he adds, " 'Let him live! Let him hide himself in outward honor, if he may!' " These bits of repetition are a small matter, but they make a contribution to the emotional intensity of these chapters. In chapter twelve, as we have already noted, Pearl three times asks Dimmesdale whether he will stand with her and her mother on the scaffold. We have also observed the frequent repetition in chapter fifteen of Pearl's two questions: what does the scarlet letter mean? and why does the minister hold his hand over his heart? Twice, in this chapter, she asks about the meaning of the letter, and four times she asks about the minister's hand. In chapter seventeen, Dimmesdale says to Hester, " 'I cannot forgive thee!' " Twice in the next paragraph, she cries, " 'Thou shalt forgive me!' " And twice a few lines later she asks, " 'Wilt thou forgive me?' " The minister responds, " 'I do forgive you, Hester. . . . I freely forgive you now. . . . May God forgive us both!' " Another small detail, but an effective one. At several other points in *The Scarlet Letter* a word, or a phrase, or a particular figure of speech is repeated to intensify the scene. In one sentence, in chapter nine, a five-fold parallel structure is used—a series of *if* clauses—with a surprisingly rhythmic result, the more so because it is not Hawthorne's habit to write such complicated sentences. [vi, 176-77] We may not entirely agree with Leon H. Vincent that "In Hawthorne there are no wasted or superfluous sentences, not even a word in excess."[7] From a twentieth-century point of view, he is often a little wordy. We must nevertheless acknowledge his skill with words and particularly his ability to arouse emotion through various artistic devices, one of which is certainly rhythm.

Half a hundred examples from *The Scarlet Letter* could be quoted to illustrate Hawthorne's use of contrast. We have already looked at several examples from his other works, and half a dozen from this novel will serve:

> There he stood, with a border of grizzled locks beneath his skull-cap; while his gray eyes, accustomed to the shaded light of his study, were winking, like those of Hester's infant, in the unadulterated sunshine. [vi, 91]

Here we have a double contrast: the young and the old on the one hand and shadow and sunshine on the other. A more typical Hawthorne contrast is the following:

> . . . to barter the transitory pleasures of the world for the heavenly hope that was to assume brighter substance as life grew dark around her, and which would gild the utter gloom with final glory. [vi, 318]

Or this glimpse of Hester:

> As if there were a withering spell in the sad letter, her beauty, the warmth and richness of her womanhood, departed, like fading sunshine; and a gray shadow seemed to fall across her. [vi, 306]

---

[7] *American Literary Masters* (Boston, Houghton Mifflin Co., 1906), p. 297.

Hawthorne often contrasts up and down, high and low, as he does here in a rather complex image of Dimmesdale:

> To the high mountain peaks of faith and sanctity he would have climbed, had not the tendency been thwarted by the burden, whatever it might be, of crime or anguish, beneath which it was his doom to totter. It kept him down, on the level with the lowest; him, the man of ethereal attributes, whose voice the angels might have listened to and answered! [VI, 203-204]

And finally, an eloquent but very complex contrast:

> Her needlework was seen on the ruff of the Governor; military men wore it on their scarfs, and the minister on his band; it decked the baby's little cap; it was shut up to be mildewed and moulder away in the coffins of the dead. But it is not recorded that, in a single instance, her skill was called in aid to embroider the white veil which was to cover the pure blushes of a bride. [VI, 117]

Certainly neither the subtle nor the obvious contrasts in this passage need explanation. In passing, we should remember the contrast offered by the two exits of Hester from the prison: the first time with fear and shame; the second with "a kind of lurid triumph."

We may now turn to the matter of color. *The Scarlet Letter* is undoubtedly the most colorful of Hawthorne's novels—but the color is always red. Lewis E. Gates says that this book is "done in deeply glowing colours against the dark, sullen background of the Puritan temperament."[8] He is generalizing here, and speaking of the indirect color of the novel. There is a great deal of direct color, too. We noted above that the phrase "the scarlet letter" is used about ninety times. This, alone, would lend color to the story. But we find that red in one form or another (red, scarlet, crimson, rose, etc.) is actually mentioned more than thirty times aside from its connection with Hester's token. Black, obviously, is the next most frequently mentioned hue. Gold, often in relation to

---

[8] *Studies and Appreciations*, p. 97.

the embroidery on the letter, is next. There is some gray, a little green, and a scattering of blue, yellow, brown, violet, and purple,—much less color, except for the red, than in *The Blithedale Romance* or *The House of the Seven Gables*. The red dominates, and against the black, as well as against "the dark, sullen background of the Puritan temperament," sets the color note of the book. There is an interesting point, already mentioned in the discussion of structure. In each of the parts A, D, and G of the novel—the three scaffold sections—fifty percent of the color words used are red. In parts B and E—the two sections dealing with Pearl and Hester—seventy percent of the color words are red. There is a balance here which strengthens the structural division. The more one delves into *The Scarlet Letter*—or, for that matter, into any of Hawthorne's better works—the more he recognizes an almost uncanny skill in organization. There is nothing intangible, however, in the color of this novel. It is red. Or rather, it is scarlet. (And Hawthorne should be praised for his choice of words. "The Red Letter" would be less effective than "The Scarlet Letter.") The use of red, the age-old symbol of adultery, is of course appropriate.

Attention was called, sometime back, to Hawthorne's frequent use of spots of light. In none of the novels are they seen to better advantage than in *The Scarlet Letter*. The sunlight is bright in the first and last scaffold scenes, and an unnatural glow illuminates the scaffold in chapter twelve. Sunshine plays an important role in this story as it does in many of Hawthorne's works. One of the chapters is called "A Flood of Sunshine." Except in the minister's study and in the market-place on the night of Dimmesdale's vigil, there is no artificial light in the book. The "bright morning sun" in the market-place is so intense that the baby "turned aside its face from the too vivid light of day." Mr. Wilson notes that Dimmesdale objects to having Hester "'lay open her heart's secrets in such broad daylight.'" Glaring sunlight brightens the Governor's Hall so that it "glittered and sparkled as if diamonds had been flung against it." In the forest, "a gleam of flickering sunshine might now and then be seen at its solitary play along the path," and when Pearl is playing by herself, the "light lingered about the lonely child." The sun goes under a cloud, but when Hester removes her scarlet letter and cap, it blazes forth again:

> All at once, as with a sudden smile of heaven, forth burst the sunshine, pouring a very flood into the obscure forest, gladdening each green leaf, transmuting the yellow fallen ones to gold, and gleaming adown the gray trunks of the solemn trees. [vi, 293]

Just before the minister mounts the scaffold to make his public confession, "The sun, but little past its meridian, shone down upon the clergyman, and gave a distinctness to his figure." These are a few of the bright, well-lighted spots in the novel.

In chapter twelve, the middle chapter, there is a moving light, which reminds us of the lighted lantern in "The Wives of the Dead." Old Mr. Wilson, who has been "praying at the bedside of some dying man," is walking home and carrying a lantern to help him in the dark night:

> It threw a gleam of recognition on here a post, and there a garden-fence, and here a latticed window-pane, and there a pump, with its full trough of water, and here, again, an arched door of oak, with an iron knocker and a rough log for the doorstep. The Reverend Mr. Dimmesdale noted all these minute particulars, even while firmly convinced that the doom of his existence was stealing onward, in the footsteps which he now heard; and that the gleam of the lantern would fall upon him in a few moments more, and reveal his long-hidden secret. [vi, 214]

Mr. Wilson does not see Dimmesdale, although the younger preacher imagines them speaking to each other. Mr. Wilson and his lantern pass on:

> The venerable Father Wilson continued to step slowly onward, looking carefully at the muddy pathway before his feet, and never once turning his head towards the guilty

platform. When the light of the glimmering lantern had faded quite away, the minister discovered, by the faintness which came over him, that the last few minutes had been a crisis of terrible anxiety. [vi, 215-16]

In this passage Hawthorne not only creates a moving light-spot of considerable effectiveness, but he also shows us the working of Dimmesdale's mind and conscience by noting the care with which the minister's eyes follow the light. It is in this same chapter, a few pages later, that Hawthorne paints a picture of the most memorable light in the book, the light cast by a meteor:

So powerful was its radiance, that it thoroughly illuminated the dense medium of cloud betwixt the sky and earth. The great vault brightened like the dome of an immense lamp. It showed the familiar scene of the street, with the distinctness of midday, but also with the awfulness that is always imparted to familiar objects by an unaccustomed light. The wooden houses, with their jutting stories and quaint gable peaks; the doorsteps and thresholds, with the early grass springing up about them; the garden plots, black with freshly turned earth; the wheel-track, little worn, and, even in the market-place, margined with green on either side,— all were visible, but with a singularity of aspect that seemed to give another moral interpretation to the things of this world than they had ever borne before. And there stood the minister, with his hand over his heart; and Hester Prynne, with the embroidered letter glimmering on her bosom; and little Pearl, herself a symbol, and the connecting link between those two. They stood in the noon of that strange and solemn splendor, as if it were the light that is to reveal all secrets, and the daybreak that shall unite all who belong to one another. [vi, 220-21]

This is the highest point, I think, and the brightest spot in the novel, and it stands, incidentally, on the middle page of the book (omitting "The Custom House" and "Conclusion").

The sound-pattern of *The Scarlet Letter*, though important and impressive, can be dealt with briefly. It can best be described as thunder and lightning. The thunder is the "tremulously sweet, rich, deep, and broken" voice of Dimmesdale. The lightning is a combined sound made up of Dimmesdale's occasional high pitches, Pearl's "eldrich scream" and her impish laugh, and a few other moments of laughter in the book. When the Puritan children taunt Pearl, Hawthorne says that "she screamed and shouted, too, with a terrific volume of sound." When she is playing on the grave-stones, "the clear, wild laughter of a young child's voice" can be heard. It is her "light, airy, childish laugh" that tells Dimmesdale of the presence of Pearl and Hester near the scaffold at night. And three times after that, while the mother, father, and child are together on the scaffold, Pearl's laugh cuts through the silence. When Hester and Pearl are in the market-place at the time of the election festivities, the little girl "broke continually into shouts of wild, inarticulate, and sometimes piercing music." Twice the shrill, cackling laugh of Mistress Hibbins echoes Pearl's laughter. Even Dimmesdale laughs " 'in bitterness and agony of heart, at the contrast between what I seem and what I am! And Satan laughs at it!' " Perhaps the most penetrating sound in the novel is the minister's scream while he is standing on the scaffold at night:

> ... an outcry that went pealing through the night, and was beaten back from one house to another, and reverberated from the hills in the background; as if a company of devils, detecting so much misery and terror in it, had made a plaything of the sound, and were bandying it to and fro.... The shriek had perhaps sounded with a far greater power to his own startled ears than it actually possessed. The town did not awake; or, if it did, the drowsy slumberers mistook the cry either for something frightful in a dream, or for the noise of witches; whose voices, at that period, were often heard to pass over the settlements or lonely cottages, as they rode with Satan through the air. [vi, 212]

But for the most part, Dimmesdale's voice is "sweet, tremulous, but powerful." Time and time again Hawthorne comments on the strength of the minister's deep and sombre tones. When Hester stands in the market-place during the election sermon, she cannot hear the words Dimmesdale is speaking, but she can hear the sound of his voice, which Hawthorne calls "this vocal organ":

> Now she caught the low undertone, as of the wind sinking down to repose itself; then ascended with it, as it rose through progressive gradations of sweetness and power, until its volume seemed to envelop her with an atmosphere of awe and solemn grandeur. And yet, majestic as the voice sometimes became, there was forever in it an essential character of plaintiveness. A loud or low expression of anguish,—the whisper, or the shriek, as it might be conceived, of suffering humanity, that touched a sensibility in every bosom! At times this deep strain of pathos was all that could be heard, and scarcely heard, sighing amid a desolate silence. But even when the minister's voice grew high and commanding,—when it gushed irrepressibly upward,—when it assumed its utmost breadth and power, so overfilling the church as to burst its way through the solid walls and diffuse itself in the open air,—still, if the auditor listened intently, and for the purpose, he could detect the same cry of pain. What was it? The complaint of a human heart, sorrow laden, perchance guilty, telling its secret, whether of guilt or sorrow, to the great heart of mankind; beseeching its sympathy or forgiveness,—at every moment,—in each accent,—and never in vain! It was this profound and continual undertone that gave the clergyman his most appropriate power. [vi, 353]

How wise it is of Hawthorne to put Hester outside the church, so that she is not able to hear the words of the sermon or to follow its meaning. Hawthorne, separating meaning from form, is apparently conscious of the emotional value of form alone, and uses it to good advantage in this passage. The thunder and lightning are again mixed in Dimmesdale's last public address, his confession. He speaks to the people of New England "with a voice that rose over them, high, solemn, and majestic,—yet always had a tremor through it, and sometimes a shriek." The sound-pattern is complete. It is always the deep rumble of the minister's voice accented by the brilliancy of his shrieks or the laughter and shrieking of Pearl.

So much for *The Scarlet Letter*. Much more might be said about it. There are other motifs that could be traced; other passages of fine prose that could be analyzed; other spots of light or flashes of color that could be pointed out. But we have seen enough to enable us to figure out the rest for ourselves.

8. Use of Selection

"Direct experience is only the raw material of literature. A cry of pain from a soul in torment is not literature any more than a bird's song is a musical composition or a sunset is a picture. Raw actuality is not art. . . . It is one of the paradoxes of literature that sincere and intense emotion does not seem sincere and intense to the reader until it has been fired in the furnace of artistic creation."—RALPH PHILIP BOAS, *The Study and Appreciation of Literature.*

———— •••• ————

"ART," SAYS Henry James, "is essentially selection. . . ."[1] The difference between nature and art, then, is largely a matter of selection. Structure, of course, is necessary to art and is one of the means of distinguishing good art from bad. But even structure, in the last analysis, is based on selection. The amateur snap-shot usually falls short of art because it lacks this important element. A picture of Old Faithful may be very interesting to the person who takes it, and possibly to a few others, but it is not necessarily a work of art. The inexperienced photographer, when he takes the picture, wants a good likeness of the geyser. The chances are that he gives very little thought to background, or lighting (unless he is very camera-conscious), or composition, or even the suitability of the subject to camera-craft. The professional photographer, if he is an artist, thinks about these things and carefully selects a camera-angle which will assure the best background; he arranges the lights or waits for a time when natural light is just right; he

---

[1] *The Art of Fiction* (Boston, DeWolfe and Fiske Co., n.d.), p. 75.

gets close to his subject or far away from it, and he arranges his subject, in so far as he can, to assure good composition; and he does not photograph something that will not make a good photograph. Because of the mechanical factor in photography, the photographer has less opportunity to select than the painter. This may be the reason why photography has never been the true art that painting is. The painter, if he is not satisfied with the shape of a natural tree, can change it. He can alter the colors, or the light-and-shade, or the position, as well as the shape and form of his subject—if he is painting from nature. If he is not painting from nature, he is absolutely free to do as he wishes. In any case, his powers of selection are limited only by his artistic imagination.

The painter, the sculptor, the musician, the architect, and the writer can and must practice selection. Perhaps no other artist has as much liberty to select as the writer. He recognizes no limitations in time or space. Everything in the known world or the unknown is grist for his mill, as long as he expresses it in terms of human experience. But he cannot write everything about all things at once. He must select. In fiction, the process of selection is almost endless. The right characters must be selected, the characters which can best convey the idea the author is trying to express. Certain aspects of the characters' personalities must be selected, and certain parts of their whole lives. Certain details must be selected to convey those personalities and experiences. And finally, the right words must be selected to make the details most vivid. So it is with the situation around which the story centers, and the setting, and the mood, and the theme of the story. Only when all this selection has been made—much of which may be unconscious or instinctive—has the story a chance of being a work of art. But in every work of art, whether fiction or painting or music or whatever the medium may be, selection will be apparent.

We cannot leave a consideration of Hawthorne the artist until we glance, however briefly, at selection in his work.

One of the results of selection, a result which the thorough-going realists often consider evil, is that *possibility* replaces *probability*. This is likely to be true of Hawthorne who, in spite of himself, is a romanticist rather than a realist. If a thing is possible, Hawthorne does not ask whether it is probable, and he is willing to stretch matters a little to make it possible. He does not care how great the odds are against him. This is true of most artists who are not bending over backward to be realistic. Rembrandt, for example, in paint-ing "Dr. Tulp's Anatomy Lesson," was not disturbed by the fact that five of the seven students who are looking on are huddled together on one side of the patient, and in a position whereby they interfere with the light. It is improbable that they would stand in this manner; it is more likely that they would have surrounded the operating-table, or at least have gotten out of the light. The grouping is improbable, but it is possible. It is equally improbable that the figures at the Last Supper would all sit on one side of a long table, as Leonardo paints them, but it is possible. It is unlikely that Diana hunted without clothes, as Goujon, Macmonnies, St. Gaudens, Man-ship, and other sculptors have pictured her, but it could hap-pen. It is improbable—to get back to Hawthorne—that Chillingworth would turn up in the market-place at Boston on the very day that Hester is exposed to public gaze on the scaffold. But it is possible; and Hawthorne selects that one day. The same kind of selection is seen in "My Kinsman, Major Molineux," where the nephew happens to come to see his uncle on the night in which he is being driven out of town in disgrace. The odds are against this occurrence, but it could happen. The little fantasy, "David Swan," illustrates the same thing. The author chooses a certain day in the life of David for his memorable nap,—the day on which the rich man's carriage breaks down, the little girl's garter slips, and the thieves are thirsty. These things all have to happen within the same period of about an hour. And furthermore they have to happen in the same place. Selection, again! That

Phoebe should return to the house of the seven gables at the same time Hepzibah and Clifford return from their flight is another example of selection. That Coverdale should choose a hotel next door to Zenobia's lodging-place; that Giovanni Guasconti should choose a boarding-house overlooking Rappaccini's garden; that Rachel, the beautiful daughter in "The Vision of the Fountain," should have "left home for boarding-school the morning after I arrived, and returned the day before my departure"; that the little cottage in "The Ambitious Guest" should be spared by the land-slide; that Priscilla should happen to come to Blithedale; or that Hilda should happen to return to Traitor's Leap just in time to see Donatello kill the model—these incidents are all a matter of chance and consequently, from our point of view, a matter of selection.

"The Minister's Black Veil" first appeared some fourteen years before *The Scarlet Letter*. In spite of the many differences between the two stories, there is an obvious aesthetic similarity. There is also a similarity in the characters of Hooper and Dimmesdale and in the moral significance of the two works. I think the relation between these stories interestingly illuminates the question of selection. In the short story, Hawthorne presents the character of the minister in a rather abstract situation. In the place of a real plot there is merely a moral problem. We know that Hawthorne was very much interested in the problem of secret sin and guilt, and it is conceivable that, after dwelling on it for some years, he decided to clothe it in a more complete plot and embody it, along with other narrative details, in a novel. We can see selection at work on a grand scale. Hooper's crime is unknown; Dimmesdale's is an unpardonable sin. Hooper has no partner to share his ignominy and punishment; Dimmesdale has Hester. Hooper has only his own conscience to force a breakdown and confession—which never occurs; Dimmesdale has Chillingworth in addition. Careful selection is evident in these differences. At no time in *The Scarlet Letter* does Hawthorne describe or discuss the crime itself. A modern realist would undoubtedly suggest it, if not picture it; but Hawthorne, concerned not with the act but only with its consequences, omits it from the story. This is certainly selection, and a kind of selection (as it always is in true art) which accurately reflects the writer's style, temperament, and purpose.

One weakness in *The Marble Faun* is a lack of selection. There is a little, of course. There has to be some selection in a story as widespread in characters and action as this novel. But there is not enough. Hawthorne does not eliminate enough detail. There is too much guide-book and not enough novel. With so slight a plot, he should not have tried to cover so much ground. The whole Monte Beni part of the book could profitably have been eliminated, I think. The story is loose; it is not compact because there has not been enough, or perhaps the right kind of, selection. It is easy to criticize and hard to write a good novel. I cannot suggest how *The Marble Faun* might be improved; but I think I am right in saying that it lacks selection.

Hawthorne's caution in the selection of details is shown in "The Birthmark," where he gives the mark the form of a small hand. Any shape would do. It might have been round or heart-shaped, or of indefinite shape; but wisely and with the true artist's sense of economy as well as effectiveness, he chooses the hand. This enables him to extend the depth of the blemish until the hand clutches Georgianna's heart, and to include, at the end of the story, the symbolic sentence, "The fatal hand had grappled with the mystery of life, and was the bond by which an angelic spirit kept itself in union with a mortal frame." The appropriateness of the miniature-portrait in "Sylph Etherege" and of the miniatures and full-length portrait in *The House of the Seven Gables* are other examples of well-selected details. Faith's pink hair-ribbon in "Young Goodman Brown" has been mentioned. It is a colorful prefiguration of the bloody baptism at the end of the story. A blue or a yellow ribbon would be as decorative, but only a pink one fits neatly into the total pattern. Mother Digby's pipe, in "Feathertop," is a good detail, as is the fluttering black veil of Mr. Hooper. The aesthetic appropriateness of Hester's scarlet letter has already been seen. The butterfly in "The Artist of the Beautiful" is an excellent suggestion. Owen Warland might have worked on a jeweled flower or a star, but he wants something that moves. It might have been a small mechanical figure that walks or gestures, or a bird, or any other insect. The butterfly meets all the requirements. It is a perfect object for minute and painstaking labor; it is beautiful; and it flies. Thus the pictorial movement at the end of the story is made possible. And, more important than all, the butterfly can be destroyed by a baby's hand. No other object would serve so well the author's aesthetic and moral purposes.

In characterization, Hawthorne, for the most part, shows restraint and a fine sense of selection. As Lewis E. Gates points out, he does not picture his characters with an abundance of detail or probe deeply into their moral and emotional backgrounds.[2] He limits characterization to a few well-selected details and to what Bliss Perry calls the "indirect method of character-delineation,"[3] whereby a figure is described in terms of his effect on others, a method which demands the omission of trivial details. Not only is there selection shown in the actual painting of characters, but there is even greater selection shown in the choosing of particular characters to carry the plot or the meaning of a story.

---

[2] Speaking of Donatello, Clifford, and Dimmesdale, Gates says: "Neither in these characters nor in any others is there an attempt at thoroughness or minuteness of realization, or at any delicate complication of motives or at scientific analysis. Hawthorne keeps his characterization carefully free from the intricacies of actual life, and preserves uncontaminate the large outlines and glowing colours of his simplified men and women. Even in speech the people of his stories are nicely unreal; his workmen are choice in their English, and his children lisp out sentences that are prettily modeled. Here, as so often, Hawthorne cares nothing for crude fact."—*Studies and Appreciations* (New York, Macmillan Co., 1900), p. 100.

[3] *A Study of Prose Fiction* (Boston, Houghton Mifflin Co., 1902), p. 104.

A simple and obvious example of this is Ernest in "The Great Stone Face," a man who is a philosopher and thus capable of drawing out the significance of the story, and a man who not only looks like the stone face but who is able also to hear its warnings and take its advice. Peter Goldthwaite's temperament is admirably suited to a search for a treasure which is not there. Polly Gookin, as well as Feathertop himself, has just the right amount of naïveté and vanity to motivate the outcome. The children in "The Snow Image" have just the right amount and kind of imagination to make their snow-child come alive, and their father has the lack of imagination which will bring about its destruction. Major Molineux's nephew is old enough to have the courage and young enough to have the curiosity and stubbornness necessary to keep his story going. How different the story would have to be if Robin were fifteen or twenty-one instead of eighteen years old. Giovanni Guasconti has just the right age and the right personality to fall in love with Rappaccini's daughter; and Professor Baglioni is just jealous enough of Rappaccini's success to let Giovanni and Beatrice destroy themselves;—to say nothing of Rappaccini himself. Owen Warland's skill and fortitude are coupled with just the right amount of simplicity and emotional instability to make his accomplishment and his tragedy possible. Were Hester more or less courageous and independent than she is, the story would be different. If Zenobia or Miriam had a greater or a lesser amount of self-confidence and beauty, their stories would have to be different. What if Chillingworth had poor health and weak will-power? What if Hepzibah had courage? What if Coverdale were willing to be reformed? The qualities of all these characters are obvious, of course, *in good stories*. But we must not forget that it is partly Hawthorne's ability to select these qualities that makes the stories good.

Hawthorne leans heavily upon contrast, in characterization as elsewhere. He often seems to select characters for their contrasting qualities, the good and the bad, or the worldly and the simple, or the wise and the stupid,—and frequently these qualities in combination. From a long list of pairs of contrasting characters, a few of the more obvious will serve. Among the men: Giovanni and Rappaccini; Elliston and Roderick in "Egotism; or the Bosom-Serpent"; Owen Warland and Peter Hovenden; Hutchinson and Lincoln in "Edward Randolph's Portrait"; Edward Hamilton and the mythical Edgar Vaughan in "Sylph Etherege"; Ethan Brand and Bartram; Ernest and the two men, General Blood-and-Thunder and Old Stoney Phiz; Adam and Gascoigne in "The Lily's Quest"; Clifford and Jaffray; Dimmesdale and Chillingworth; Coverdale and Hollingsworth; and Donatello and Kenyon. Among the women there are not so many, probably because there are fewer women in Hawthorne: Edith and the old maid in "The White Old Maid"; Mother Digby and Polly Gookin in "Feathertop"; Phoebe and Hepzibah; Zenobia and Priscilla; Miriam and Hilda; and, we might add, Hester and Pearl. Relying on broad, sweeping, inclusive traits to describe his characters, Hawthorne can bring out the virtue in one man by showing the vice in another, or the smoothness of one and the roughness of another, or the brightness and the dullness, or any other pair of contrasting qualities.

Just as this method of broad characterization is one of the surest marks of a high degree of selectivity in Hawthorne, and one of his strengths, so it is one of his weaknesses. It results in characters which tend to become types. There is a noticeable lack of variety in Hawthorne's characters, a great deal of repetition. We have Peter Goldthwaite and Dominicus Pike in "Mr. Higginbotham's Catastrophe"; Hooper and Dimmesdale; little Annie, Ilbrahim in "The Gentle Boy," and the children in "The Snow Image"; the villains—Chillingworth, Hollingsworth, Dr. Heidegger, Professor Baglioni, and Rappaccini; the upright and rather colorless young men —Kenyon, Coverdale, Holgrave, and Adam in "The Lily's Quest"; the witches—Mother Digby, Mistress Hibbins, and the old crone in "The Hollow of the Three Hills"; the sweet, innocent young girls—Priscilla, Hilda, Phoebe, Alice Vane, Lillian Fay in "The Lily's Quest," Goodman Brown's Faith, Georgianna, and Margaret and Mary in "The Wives of the Dead"; the colorful women of the world—Zenobia and Miriam—(Hester, I think, cannot be classed with these two). There are other groups of similar characters, but these listed are sufficient to make the point. Hawthorne loses as well as gains by his process of selection in characterization. But so, for that matter, do most writers. And in the field of painting, we find that Leonardo's women all look pretty much alike, and so do the men of the Bellinis, and the figures of Rembrandt, Rubens, Frans Hals, and even Titian and Raphael. In character creation and portrayal, artists, whether painters or writers, tend to select characteristics which rapidly establish types.

This same fault—if it is that—can be seen in Hawthorne's settings. New England and Italy furnish the background for practically all of his stories, long and short. But Poe is not much better in this respect, nor is O. Henry, Irving, Howells, Melville, nor de Maupassant, Hugo, Dickens, nor any but a very few of the great story-tellers. Their settings are limited in time and space by their experience and their interests. Hawthorne's settings are well selected, for the most part, and are suitable to the stories which they surround. He says in the Preface to *The Marble Faun* that Italy is a good site for this tale because of its romantic nature. It *is* a good site, but it is not as necessary to the novel as early Boston is to *The Scarlet Letter*. It is probable that the story of Hester and Dimmesdale could have taken place in no other setting. Early nineteenth-century Massachusetts is a well-chosen background for *The Blithedale Romance*. The Brook Farm episode, of course, colors the reader's appreciation of this book just as it did Hawthorne's creative imagination. *The House of the Seven Gables* fits well into its background, although this story might conceivably occur in any land and at any time which offers old houses and old families. But the house it-self is a perfect selection.

We have noted the appropriateness of the market-place with its scaffold in *The Scarlet Letter*. Here Hawthorne has chosen with great care and has built the details of the setting into the structure of the story. The entire action takes place in or very close to Boston; there is a strong unity of place. Except for the brief flight of Clifford and Hepzibah, the action of *Seven Gables* is even more tightly bound: it all happens in and around the house. *The Blithedale Romance* is confined to the farm, Boston, and a little town: only eight of the thirty-nine chapters are set away from the farm. In *The Marble Faun*, twelve of the fifty chapters are set away from Rome and its environs, and within the thirty-eight Roman chapters there are many different backgrounds. I am not trying to argue that a novel should have a single setting or that the fewer the settings the better. I believe, however, that Hawthorne has most success when he has most unity of place. It is this unity that gives much of the power to *The Scarlet Letter* and *Seven Gables*.

The setting of "Ethan Brand" is one of the finest in the short stories. The dark night throws the glow of the fire into high relief, and the loneliness of the place stresses the horror of the action. Had Ethan killed himself in another place and under different circumstances the story would be looser and weaker. The particular arrangement of rooms, in relation to the fire-light, makes the setting of "The Wives of the Dead" as fortunate a choice as the "hollow basin, almost mathemati-cally circular" is for "The Hollow of the Three Hills." Attention has already been called to the pastoral charm of "The Lily's Quest" and the dark, meandering streets in "My Kins-man, Major Molineux." The Arcadian simplicity of Blithe-dale; the "legendary interest" of the church with its funeral bell in "The Wedding Knell"; the loneliness of a large city in "Wakefield"; the "mountain lake, deep, bright, clear, and calmly beautiful" in "The Great Carbuncle"; the "dim, old fashioned chamber, festooned with cobwebs and besprinkled with antique dust" in "Dr. Heidegger's Experiment"; the strange and artificial splendor of the laboratory in "The Birthmark"; the haunted forest in "Young Goodman Brown"; and the cold, damp cave in "The Man of Adamant"—these and many other settings are all different and all carefully selected for their respective stories. Hawthorne is adept at selection, and when he exercises his powers, he produces fine, artistic tales; when he fails to select, he weakens his art.

With very few exceptions, Hawthorne's stories all have the same general mood. They are sombre—though often resplendent with color; they are serious, if not tragic; and they tend to be weird, mysterious, and supernatural. Illustrations of these qualities are scarcely necessary. Occasionally, in a minor character such as Uncle Venner, or Dominicus Pike in "Mr. Higginbotham's Catastrophe," there is a touch of comedy. Sometimes there is a hint of satire, as in "The Devil in Manuscript" or "Feathertop" or as in many of the frieze-stories. On the whole, though, Hawthorne is serious. He is, according to some critics, earnestly preoccupied with morality —a matter not within the province of this study. As Henry James says, "We are discussing the Art of Fiction; questions of art are questions (in the widest sense) of execution; questions of morality are quite another affair . . ."[4] We need not argue whether Hawthorne is moralist or artist; he may be, and probably is, both. He is certainly not a propagandist. Art may be moral and still remain art, as long as it does not become propaganda. If many artists, including Michelangelo, Leonardo, Giotto, and many of the medieval sculptors were propagandists (in one sense), with few exceptions they were propagandists from necessity (monetary) and not from choice. In general, art and propaganda do not mix. Hawthorne was undoubtedly concerned with the problem of sin

---

[4] *The Art of Fiction*, p. 81.

and redemption, but it is not likely that he wrote his stories or novels for sermons. Neither external nor internal evidence supports such a claim. If he tended to select moral problems, it is because they interested him. From the present point of view, Hawthorne's moral interest counts in his favor, because it means that he was a fine artist in spite of this. Wherein the mood of his stories would be different if he were not so concerned with the problem of sin, I do not know. That is a little like asking: what would Hawthorne's stories be like if someone else had written them?

9. Conclusion

"What we seek and enjoy in art, what makes our heart leap up and ravishes
our admiration, is the life, the movement, the passion, the fire, the feeling of
the artist; that alone gives us the supreme criterion for distinguishing works
of true art and false art, inspiration, and failure. Passion and feeling cover a
multitude of sins. If they are lacking, nothing can take their place."
—BENEDETTO CROCE, *Problems of Aesthetics.*

HAWTHORNE, living in America in the first half of the
nineteenth century, found his countrymen, on the
whole, unfriendly towards art and artists. In Europe, particularly in France, romantic art was thriving and much
appreciated; but in America, conditions were unfavorable.
We were too close to the pains of our birth.

The colonists were both practical and mystical. The hard-
ships of their lives accentuated the first characteristic, and
the fervor of their religion stimulated the second. Whatever
beauty they desired, at least consciously, was achieved either
in their religion or in the few kinds of art that fulfilled practical needs: the painting of portraits, of stage coaches or
signs; the carving of wooden figure-heads for New England
ships, or stone monuments for graves; the building of houses
only slightly modified from their Tudor models; the ham-
mering of decorative iron; or the writing of political or
religious tracts.[1]

Out of such a background Hawthorne sprang, and under
conditions not much better he studied and practiced his art.
It is true that he had available as models all the masterpieces

---

[1] Helen Dwan Schubert, "Hawthorne, a Puritan Artist" (Master's thesis, Cornell
University, 1939), p. 6.

of world literature, just as Hugo, Dickens, Thackeray, and Gogol did. But it is also true that Hawthorne came from a line of Puritans who scorned art; that his American contemporaries were not very art-conscious; that he had little encouragement to learn about art; and that in the visual arts there were not many available examples for his consideration. His Puritan background taught him that only useful art was not sinful. From this standpoint, then, most so-called fine art was a bad influence. This was an age in which Christopher Cranch, the painter, could write:

> In this country Art just lives—it is far from flourishing. The artist has need of all his courage and patience to stick to his vocation. . . . Here, surrounded by a selfish, commercial, money-making, rushing, driving, and wholly conventional community, what can an artist do?[2]

There were some pictures and statues in Salem and Boston during Hawthorne's years, but very few really good works. Sophia Hawthorne's interest in painting meant that there were works of art in their home, and she knew Allston as Hawthorne knew Thompson. But in spite of all this, the opportunity to see works of art and to talk about them was limited. Yet Hawthorne was interested in art. He read about it whenever he could; and in England, France, and Italy he spent a great deal of time looking at buildings, paintings, and sculptures, as we know from the note-books. Although his taste was never very well developed, he realized this and constantly tried to improve it.

Theoretically, as his taste and critical judgment improved, his skill as a literary artist should have improved too. But this did not happen. From his comments in the note-books we can easily infer that the highest point of his aesthetic appreciation, taste, and judgment was reached while he was in Italy in 1858-1859. But *The Marble Faun,* which grew out of

---

[2] From a letter to the Misses Meyers, June 22, 1851, cited in Leonora Cranch Scott, *The Life and Letters of Christopher Pearse Cranch* (Boston, Houghton Mifflin Co., 1917), p. 183.

his Italian experience, is, I think, the weakest of his novels. From the point of view of this study, the novels can be ranked *The Scarlet Letter, The House of the Seven Gables, The Blithedale Romance,* and lastly *The Marble Faun,*—the order in which the books were published. In other words, Hawthorne's skill in handling form in art seems to have diminished. The fifteen years leading up to and including *The Scarlet Letter* were, from the present point of view, Hawthorne's best years. Within this period we find "Young Goodman Brown" (1835), "The Maypole of Merry Mount" and "The Minister's Black Veil" (1836), "Fancy's Show-Box," "Dr. Heidegger's Experiment," and "David Swan" (1837), "Howe's Masquerade" (1838), "The Birthmark" (1843), "The Artist of the Beautiful" and "Rappaccini's Daughter" (1844), and "Ethan Brand" and *The Scarlet Letter* (1850). As works of art, these stories are the best, not only because they are outstanding in the element of form—as I have been trying to point out—but also because they have what Croce calls, in the heading to this chapter, "the life, the movement, the passion, the fire, the feeling of the artist." If stories, or any other works of art, are lacking in these things, as Croce goes on to say, "nothing can take their place"—not even form. Of course, some of Hawthorne's other stories also have both form and feeling. (Unfortunately for my argument, "The Snow-Image" is also dated 1850, and this is one of the weaker stories; and "The Hollow of the Three Hills," "My Kinsman, Major Molineux," and "Roger Malvin's Burial" precede 1835. Chance will have to explain these discrepancies.) We can safely say that Hawthorne developed and that his powers as an artist increased up to *The House of the Seven Gables,*—with *The Scarlet Letter* as the fullest and finest example of his artistry.

In his best tales and novels, Hawthorne works as an artist works. He is conscious of aesthetic structure and builds his stories around neat patterns. He employs mass, line, movement, contrast, and variety for the creation of artistic effects.

He is rhythmical. He produces stimuli which evoke vivid images in color, in light-and-shade, and in sound. He uses selection with a fine discrimination. He does all this in spite of his Puritan background and his relative ignorance of art principles. Perhaps we must conclude that his ability is somewhat instinctive and unconscious, but it is none the less artistic. Perhaps Hawthorne works even better than he knows —but so do most artists.

Index